PRAISE FOR *INTENTIONING*

....

From the woman who has spent her life shifting our relationship to power, now Gloria's giving us a master class on how to channel that power and maximize the impact that is so deeply needed today, with intention! Disruption without intention is chaos, and inside the pages of *Intentioning*, you will find the hard-earned roadmap to help us all, no matter our gender, get to where our ancestors' wildest dreams imagined we'd someday arrive.

—**Nathalie Molina Niño, managing director, Known Holdings, and author of *Leapfrog***

Many books tell women what to do to succeed. *Intentioning* takes a fresh approach by helping women be more authentically who we are and appreciating our unique powers of intention . . . . The 9 Leadership Intentioning Tools are golden nuggets of actionable skills and tips you can use right away. More important, they provide new ways of thinking that will stand you in good stead throughout your life and career.

—**May Busch, CEO of Career Mastery™ and former COO of Morgan Stanley Europe**

We need this book now. This pandemic has disproportionately negatively impacted women, and we not only have ground to make up, but we must take our rightful place as more equitable partners in leadership across all sectors. Our intentions, individual and collective, will drive our actions which, in turn, will manifest outcomes.

—**Jacki Zehner, founder, ShePlace; cofounder, Women Moving Millions; former partner and managing director, Goldman Sachs**

Few books on women's leadership include intersectionality and racial justice; few books on racial justice include women's leadership. Yet the two must go forward together or neither is likely to succeed. In *Intentioning*, Gloria Feldt weaves together the case and provides examples of diverse women's experiences of intentioning: "Intend it. See it. It will happen."

—Lily D. McNair, Ph.D., eighth president and first woman
president of Tuskegee University

Gloria Feldt masterfully weaves her "Lead Like a Woman" framework into 9 Leadership Intentioning Tools. *Intentioning*'s actionable best practices deliberately position women leaders to create an equitable and more productive workplace that allows everyone to thrive. The "must-read" for every leader who is serious about positioning their organization for success in the twenty-first century!

—Dr. David G. Smith, co-author,
Athena Rising: How and Why Men Should Mentor Women
and *Good Guys: How Men Can Be Better Allies for Women in*
the Workplace

Gloria is the Meryl Streep of leadership: pitch perfect in her essaying of her destined role to inspire and energize women worldwide. Ringing with purpose and power, her words set you free to embrace your ambition, love your struggling self, and touch your deepest core within.

—Dr. Harbeen Arora, founder, G100,
Women Economic Forum (WEF), and Bioayurveda

If you're ready to leave the past behind and lead with intention, this is not only a "must-read" but also a must-follow book. Gloria is the go-to expert on "taking the lead" and this guide further highlights her knowledge and expertise as well as amplifies stories of women who've battled back, and succeeded, with intention.

—Cate Luzio, founder and CEO, Luminary

Never has there been a better time to rethink leadership after a period of intense disruption that heightened the intense challenges already faced by women and minorities. Gloria Feldt's book *Intentioning* is a fresh and liberating approach to rethinking and reaching gender parity in leadership and life.

—Juliet Scott-Croxford, CEO of Worth Media

INTENTIONING

SEX, POWER, PANDEMICS, AND HOW WOMEN WILL TAKE THE LEAD FOR (EVERYONE'S) GOOD

GLORIA FELDT

*For the frontline essential workers who gave
so selflessly during the pandemic.*

. . . .

*Intentioning
Sex, Power, Pandemics, and How Women Will Take
the Lead for (Everyone's) Good*

Published by Worth Books.

Cover Design by Bruce Gore, Gore Studio Inc.

ISBN: 978-1-63763-015-0 print
ISBN: 978-1-63763-016-7 e-book

TABLE OF CONTENTS

PART II
9 LEADERSHIP
INTENTIONING TOOLS

· · · · · · · · · · · · · · · · ·

PART III
INTENTIONING GENDER PARITY IS A
MOVEMENT...AND IT INCLUDES MEN

••••••••••••••••••

FOREWORD

By Jamia Wilson

Do you recall the first time you felt powerful in your life? Although this may seem like a simple question on the surface, the revelations this query stirred in my soul inspired me to write a children's book, *Step into Your Power*. Despite being force-fed a media and cultural narrative that promotes a limited definition of who we are as women, I always felt an intrinsic right to claim my power even if others weren't ready for it yet.

I grew up wondering whether the link between power and purpose is about a state of being or more of an active movement. The one thing I didn't question was the core and the heart of what always drove me back to my power: a sense of intention driven by values and passion. Although I remain curious about how we can all evolve our relationship with honoring our own authority, the only thing I've ever known for sure is that it lives within us in its most authentic and sacred form.

I thought about this lifelong exploration when I participated in Gloria Feldt's 2020 Take The Lead conference in Scottsdale, Arizona, over two decades after I first embraced my own sense of powerfulness. As I approached the podium in tailored business attire with a laptop in hand, I flashed back to the first time I recited poetry at a church conference in South Carolina. Although my pigtailed and white pinafore-clad self was much smaller in physical size then, I embraced an innate feeling of immense strength. I gasped in the moment with the recognition that our power and intention to make ripples and even waves in this world are our birthright. I didn't have to or need to ask permission to be enough to make change—and neither do you.

My first early brush with embracing my truth and trusting my instincts paved the way for me to trust that my ideas and my voice mattered then and now. As I looked upon a room full of "intentional leaders," I realized that each of us already possesses the power to make discernments that could advance progress, yet somehow along the way, we likely encountered derailments and distractions.

More than likely, I thought, *we had also received messages that conditioned us to question or contradict one another's truths and perspectives as women in a society without full political, social, and economic parity and justice for all.*

In that spirit, I focused my remarks on what I had learned about staying on mission, staying engaged, and making a difference. As much as I spoke to this bright and bold group of women, I discovered, dear reader, that I was also talking to and healing the part of myself that needed a reminder that my own intentions and my own experiences are essential to our understanding of who we are and what we can be, just like *yours* are and hers are.

While scanning the festive conference room, I visualized what it would mean and look like for every woman leader in the room to know, trust, and speak about the transformative power of their insights and those of one another in any environmental, political, or cultural weather.

Amplifying voices often left out of the public discourse sparks my passion because it allows us to connect through our shared experiences, learn from our differences, and bear witness.

Enlivening our intentions through our words and deeds makes the communities we represent visible and elevates our consciousness so that our recollection of history and the present is more inclusive. After I delivered the keynote, I had an epiphany. To truly claim and understand our intentions and our power, we must interrogate why we have ever questioned their presence in the first place. Nature and the animal kingdom are brilliant at staying connected to their intention—their way of being. A lion doesn't forget that he's the king of the jungle because he's burned out, but as human beings, sometimes we veer off course and need to come back to ourselves. Along the way, for many historical, systemic, and cultural reasons, we have been sometimes awkwardly, jarringly, and even traumatically pulled away from the force field of our own truth.

Growth is always power, no matter how we get there along the way. And now, instead of cowing to perfectionism or diminishing my fire because someone else can't handle the glare, I wonder, what did that interaction, that message, that failure or challenging moment teach me about how I plan to step into my power next time around with fierce intention? Intuitively, we know the way forward, but many of us (myself included) have been conditioned to seek approval, to conform to a patriarchal structure that has shown us for centuries that it doesn't work, and to reject our intrinsic knowing and our *being*.

After reading this book, I am challenging myself as I enter this next phase of my life to ask the women I meet the following question: What is your core intention and how can I and we help you get there?

As you explore Gloria's incisive and insightful book, you will see yourself and women you know. As someone who has been mentored and supported by Gloria's visionary and loving leadership for over a decade, I can assure you that you're in for a treat and you will be transformed. Gloria has taught me a lot of things, but most of all she has taught me to be ready to seize the moment with strategy and intention in the face of sunshine or a storm.

Yes, Gloria's wisdom will teach you how to be your own GPS, your wayfinder no matter what dragons you need to slay. It will provide you with the tools to take the right next step or to speak the right next words, and to find the necessary courage to do so.

Get ready, in your reflection within these pages, to meet the woman who has always resided within you—the "you" you have yet to meet as she embraces, elevates, and expands into the next level of the trailblazer she was already born to be.

This book will inspire you to discover and truly accept that each of us can play an influential role in shaping a better and brighter future together. No matter what problems we want to solve or spaces we wish to innovate, through "intentioning" we can and will understand our ability to address power imbalances, to shatter the glass and break through our blocks.

I can't wait to see you on the other side. It's our time.

••••••••••••••••••

Jamia Wilson is vice president/executive editor at Penguin Random House and former executive director and publisher at Feminist Press. Early in her career, she worked at Planned Parenthood Federation of America when Gloria was its president and CEO and has counted Gloria as a mentor ever since. Gloria, in turn, feels she has learned just as much from Jamia as she has risen in leadership while modeling the power of intentioning.

····················

IT TOOK TWO PANDEMICS TO BREAK THE BOUNDARIES THAT HAVE HELD US BACK

I'd never broken a bone in my life until I broke my wrist one sunshiny Arizona morning in January of 2020. I was ambling down a gentle mountain slope, chatting with my friend, feeling ever so grateful for the spectacular desert views.

Then *boom!* I tripped on a small, jagged rock. Instinctively I put my left hand out to catch myself. I felt the snap and instantly knew by the pain that I'd broken my wrist.

Luckily a physician was on the trail behind me. She turned my sweatshirt into a sling and walked me the rest of the way down the hill where my friend dashed to get her car to take me to the emergency room. I wryly repeated one of my favorite hard-earned leadership aphorisms: It's not the mountains that trip you up; it's the pebbles on the path.

X-rays, surgery, a sling, and then a splint and weeks of physical therapy ensued. They slowed me down but didn't deter me from the optimism that had ushered in the year. Looking back, I should have seen the fall as an omen. The year of broken bones is how I think of it now. Broken almost everything, it turns out, including boundaries of tradition and structure. A disruption of massive proportions.

But back then, I was sure 2020 was going to be epic. I loved the sound of it. The round numbers. That it was the 100th anniversary of the 19th Amendment to the Constitution codifying American women's right to vote. It was a major election year too. A moment when women were poised to crack the 25 percent mark in top leadership positions across the board. Surely then it would be easy to double that to 50 percent, per my goal and the mission of Take The Lead®, the nonprofit organization I cofounded in 2013. Our aim is full leadership intersectional gender parity by 2025. That's 70 to 150 years faster than the most optimistic projections.

We kicked off 2020 with the inaugural Power Up Conference: *Unleashing the Intentional Leader Within.* I had insisted it be held February 28 and 29 because February 29, Leap Day, is the most feminist of days. It bears that symbolism thanks to Saint Brigid, who secured a decree in 5th-century Ireland allowing women to turn the tables on tradition by asking men to marry them on that one and only day every four years.

Giving women greater agency over their life paths was the point of it all.

Then *boom* again. The week after our conference, all hell broke loose as the magnitude of the global coronavirus pandemic began to sink in. Though viruses are tiny enough to be imperceptible to the naked eye, this one was more like an impassable mountain on the road than just a pebble. It stopped the world cold for more than a year.

••

Stepping back, I could see that many pebbles had tripped me up along the personal trail I've taken. It took this mountain to put the journey in greater perspective.

••

My winding path began in small Texas towns in a culture and during a time when women weren't supposed to have aspirations beyond home, hearth, and supporting others. I learned to cover my aspirations and quiet my voice to fit in. I fell into the established pattern of early marriage and children. At 20, with two toddlers and an infant, I realized that I had no employable skills. Soon thereafter, I started community college.

It would be some time before I coined the term "intentioning"—the active form of intention—but I had been slowly and painfully developing my awareness of it even during those early days. I bet you've practiced it at some point in your life, perhaps as unconsciously as I did at first, though experience has taught me that it is so much more effective when mindfully applied to an objective or challenge that emanates from the power within and aligns with our core purpose.

Doing such purposeful work since then has been a privilege. The unifying thread for me has been women's equality, where I have been both a witness and a contributor to making historic gains. And though I've had the incredible opportunity to lead the world's largest reproductive health and advocacy nonprofit organization, Planned Parenthood Federation of America, through enormous challenges *and* had the opportunity to write bestselling books, the findings of which led me to cofound Take The Lead, I still struggle with embracing the power of my own intention. *What path would I have chosen if I had been intentional?*

I learned leadership on the job and through the school of hard knocks, not at an Ivy League university. I took opportunities that were offered, yes. I was smart and I worked hard, yes. But I never operated from a place of clarity about my intention. I accepted the locus of power outside of myself. It has taken years of self-work to bring that power source inside so I can use it to clarify and then claim and elevate my true intentions.

That's how and why I created the concept of intentioning. At first it was to help myself. Now it is intended to help you and all women identify your value and values, embrace the phenomenal power that I know you have (even if you don't see it yet), and elevate your vision and achievements to your highest intentions.

As this book unfolds, I'll make the case that female socialization around power and intention, even more than the external barriers and biases that do still remain, is the linchpin holding us back from leadership parity and equality in all forms.

Yet that same socialization has the potential to become our superpower when inculcated with intention. And we will need all our superpowers to reach gender parity because if you think about it, transforming our institutions to gender equality will be one of the most profound disruptions in recorded human history.

Intentioning the Impossible

Take The Lead started planning—or I should say, *intentioning*—our conference late in 2019. Although people told us that a meeting of that magnitude couldn't be executed so quickly, the team and our incredible Leadership Ambassador and founder of the Black Women's Collective, Felicia Davis, along with some devoted volunteers and kickass speakers, pulled it off to rave reviews, nevertheless.

Participants were effusive in their praise for the event. So many of them talked about the joy they felt in the company of newfound friends. They expressed appreciation for the diversity of the assembled group, the pervasive sense of sisterhood, and the countless opportunities they had in those two days to meet up close and personally role models they had long admired from afar. The feeling of optimism as people connected, exchanged ideas, and sparked each other to greater possibilities was palpable. An instant community formed by proximity and shared values.

Thank goodness we went ahead with what had been deemed an impossible task, because as the news of the global COVID-19 pandemic began to spread faster than the virus itself the day after the conference, life as we knew it ground to a grudging halt. Within a month fear stalked the world, the health care system was in crisis mode, and half of the country was working from home if they still had jobs. By February 2021, 5,000,000 American women, twice as many as men, were out of work either from job loss or leaving the workforce due to the pressures of caregiving responsibilities, and women's job participation fell to a 33-year low.[1] Though the gender split among new hires was almost 50/50 by May 2021,[2] the country, and especially women, still have far to go to recoup job losses from the pandemic. Given the importance of mindset, it is notable that Deloitte's Women @ Work study of 5,000 working women across 10 countries found 51 percent are feeling less optimistic about their career prospects than they were prior to the disruption of the pandemic.[3]

Beyond the unemployment numbers, the enthusiasm, determination, and energy generated by being with like-minded friends in physical community were gone.

Almost every other conference on the calendar had been cancelled. A prescient few organizers had shifted theirs to a virtual platform in the early pandemic months, using whatever cranky technology existed, but most others wrongly assumed that they would pick up where they had left off in a few weeks and simply postponed their live events.

Soon the parallel pandemic of racial injustice—a phenomenon as old as America itself—was out in the open for all to see at last. The murders by police of George Floyd and Breonna Taylor, on the heels of an increasingly evident pattern of biased brutality, triggered a widespread reckoning as people of all races took to the streets in support of the Black Lives Matter movement.

At the same time, relooks at history as the anniversary of the 19th Amendment approached revealed that although the women's suffrage movement led to the ratification of that amendment in 1920, it did not guarantee *all* women the right to vote as our history books often suggest. While the amendment declared that the right of citizens to vote could not be denied or abridged by the United States or by any state on account of sex, many women of color at the time still found themselves navigating Jim Crow laws prohibiting or suppressing their vote. Indigenous people and

Asian Americans had to wait years to get their full voting rights. And as the election cycle of 2020 proved, women (and men) of color still had to work for full access to the polls and to overcome widespread efforts to suppress their vote in certain states. We'll address this more in chapters to come.

As I ready this book for publication more than a year later, it's safe to say that none of us has been untouched or unchanged by these tandem pandemics and the economic reverberations of them. We've all had to summon the strength to do whatever was necessary to keep going, to support friends and family, to home-school our children, and to maintain businesses whether out in the public as essential workers or within the confines of our makeshift kitchen-table offices. In the wake of these monumental events, there is not only a need to continue the work for racial and gender justice, there is a profound need to *accelerate* that work.

As it turns out, the Leap Day that occurred before the pandemic lockdown and the long period of loss and suspended reality that consumed the remainder of 2020 and parts of 2021 bears as much symbolism now as it did during our PowerUp conference, for it augured the giant leap forward we are poised to take today.

··

We are in a season of disruption; we are in a season of rebirth.

··

The two have much in common. What we once thought of as normal will never be again, but both disruption and rebirth provide opportunities to normalize entirely new realities—to create purposefully and provocatively a better future for ourselves than we've ever enjoyed. Boundaries of thinking that were rigidly dictated by tradition or patriarchy can open up just like that, because in times such as these, innovations are necessary for us to survive and thrive.

Now that we are on the cusp of wrangling the pandemic to the ground and you've boldly ventured to pick this book up, my ~~hope~~ *intention* is that you are well and safe, and on your way to normalizing a new future—the future of your choice—because the positive side of massive disruptions such as COVID-19, economic crashes, and racial reckoning is that the borders that previously organized our lives and institutions are breached. Gaping holes in the prepandemic structures can now let the light of new ideas in by the power of our intentions. But as Gloria Steinem has observed, "The first problem for all of us, men and women, is not to learn, but to unlearn."

Our institutions are organisms. They have structures that can become rigid over time. But they are also like amoebas in that they can alter their shapes as needed when a change in environment coerces them to adapt and flow in new directions. Institutions tend to be resistant to change until they have no other option except to think differently. Ridding themselves of old ideas is difficult and that's what keeps them from letting new ideas in until they absolutely must. Massive disruptions such as wars, economic depressions, and pandemics force those rigid boundaries to become malleable as a sheer survival mechanism.

For instance, who would have thought two years ago that women-led countries would be recognized for managing the pandemic better than other nations? That we'd actually maintain deep, human connections through screens on our devices—the same devices that frequently threatened to isolate and divide us before? That shopping in stores would give way to shopping online at a pace four times greater than economists had predicted? Or that something called "the mirror" would turn even the smallest apartment into one's own private gym? Adaptation and change are visible in both subtle and substantial ways.

Who could have predicted that the Black Lives Matter movement, which had been growing steadily for several years, would finally explode into such a massive global movement for comprehensive racial justice in response to the murder of George Floyd? Who could have predicted that geography would cease to matter for local chapter-based organizations such as Golden Seeds, an angel investor collaborative that invests in companies led by women? Now this organization, and others like it, can connect their investor members with prospective start-up companies regardless of where they are located. That altered reality literally opens up a world of potential investor-entrepreneur connections that might not otherwise have happened. And it has increased, rather than decreased, the number of people who are able to participate in any given event.

Also consider how many law firms no longer need expensive office space or how many companies are genuinely working for the first time to turn the fine words about diversity on their websites into real actions for equity and inclusion.

Vaccines and improved treatments are enabling us to be physically together again, to great feelings of relief and the joy of hugging our loved ones. My bones are healed. But even so, few of us wish to return fully to our society's old model. What better chance will we ever have to rethink caregiving as an economic necessity and a social good? How obvious has it become that women and men can work more flexibly from home much of the time and remain just as productive as before, making the old 9-to-5 routine a relic of the past?

· ·

These moments of disruption and rebirth are the best opportunities we will ever have in the foreseeable future to create innovative new ways of living and working. *Intentioning: Sex, Power, Pandemics, and How Women Will Take the Lead for (Everyone's) Good* is a call for us not to waste this precious moment in time. If we put women at the center of the recovery, the result will be a more equitable, prosperous, and healthy society for all.

· ·

The "Lead Like a Woman" framework and the "9 Leadership Intentioning Tools" you will find in the following pages provide the roadmap for career and life successes you will need as you go forward in this changed world, whether you have to pivot your career out of necessity, want to rethink your purpose because your old one no longer has meaning for you, or you simply aim to elevate your highest and best intentions to achieve a greater purpose than you might have imagined previously.

I began writing this book before COVID-19 stopped us in our tracks because I wanted to help women of all diversities and intersectionalities embrace their phenomenal power. The power to identify and act on their intentions. The power to elevate their own lives. The power to assume leadership roles. And the power to help all women attain equality in position and pay to their male counterparts in their respective professions. The inspiration and practical tools shared in these pages are needed now more than ever.

Women *must* be at the center of the recovery if it is to be a robust and enduring one. We cannot afford to squander women's talents, especially when rebuilding a shattered economy lies in the balance. I created a hashtag that I urge you to use often until it becomes true: #**putwomenatthecenter**.

I also created the verb "intentioning" from the noun "intention" to signal action, not just thought. I wanted to indicate to you and the rest of the world that intentioning is different from having mere ambition. It's more than a state of mind. It's the conscious act of seizing the moment and creating the life and career that you want—one that benefits all of society by providing greater balance and harmony. If we set about intentioning, using all of the resources provided here, there is no end to the personal and societal good we can put into motion.

Intentioning, when understood not only by women but by all, enables companies and governing bodies to retain and accelerate women into and up through the leadership pipeline where their different experiences and perspectives can inform the positive changes we are seeking.

This book is not about a single pandemic, though COVID is the current disruption that sent the world to its knees. It's about how we lead through disruption with the help of that thought and action process I call intentioning. There will be other pandemics. There will be other massive disruptions—technologies that change how we work and live, weather events from hurricanes and tornadoes to all-out climate change, global conflicts, economic depressions, and, of course, infectious diseases. And there will be the constant individual disruptions we all face in our lives, from business setbacks to losing people we love. So the concepts and leadership intentioning tools in this book are evergreen, relevant far beyond the current turbulence.

••

By reading *Intentioning* and embracing the process, you will answer for yourself your inevitable next question: the power *to WHAT?* Because as humorist Will Rogers once said, "Even if you're on the right track, you'll get run over if you just sit there."

••

Your potential is tangible. The means to using it wisely is laid out in these chapters, which now rest in your very capable hands.

PART ONE

FROM EMBRACING POWER TO INTENTIONING THE NEXT LEVEL OF LEADERSHIP

....

CHAPTER 1

YOU'VE ALWAYS HAD THE POWER, MY DEAR

If you are a *Wizard of Oz* fan as I am, you will remember Glinda the Good Witch telling the protagonist Dorothy that all she had to do was click her heels together and she would achieve the intention that led her to have so many adventures and misadventures along the yellow brick road—that she would *finally* be able to go home to Kansas. "You always had the power, my dear," Glinda reminded her. "You just had to learn it for yourself."

As you dive into *Intentioning*, remember that my goal is to help you and women of all diversities and intersectionalities embrace your phenomenal power *TO* lead with confidence, authenticity, and joy.

Embracing your power frees you to practice elevating your intentions so you can get the lives and leadership roles you want in a healthy way. What's more, every woman's individual progress helps *all* women reach equal power, position, and pay. In turn, families rise out of poverty. The toll from economic stress on both men and women is reduced, enabling them to provide better education, nutrition, and life experiences to their children. So when I say "for everyone's good," it's true.

And there are systemic benefits too. When companies use these methods to elevate the intentions and embrace the power of their female employees, they increase retention and lower recruitment and onboarding costs, all while accelerating women's progress through the leadership pipeline.

Show me a solution to any challenge where there is a bigger payoff all around than advancing women into leadership parity with men.

I dedicated this book to those exemplars of intention: the frontline workers who sacrificed so much to care for the sick and keep essential services going and to those who suffered from or lost their lives to the horrible coronavirus. The frontline workers, who are disproportionately women and people of color, are proof positive of the public good that is so needed and can occur only when we #putwomenatthecenter.

It is further imperative that we #putwomenatthecenter of the recovery, so the rebound will be robust and the trajectory toward gender equality in leadership will be hastened, and in turn will further the evolution of a more just and prosperous world.

My mission, my passion, is to see gender parity in leadership achieved throughout every sector of business and governing in the next four years. It was a big, bold goal before the pandemic and it's a big, bold goal even now, but in many ways the path has been cleared by the storm that tore through our society. We have to stake a claim to the new territory unveiled to us in the aftermath of that storm.

For as I noted previously, disruption and rebirth have much in common. Just as power has no inherent qualities, the same can be said of the time that lies ahead of us. It will be what we make of it. What we think of as normal will never be again. But in disruption and rebirth, we can normalize new realities and create a better future more intentionally and proactively than we have ever before. Boundaries of thinking that were rigidly sealed by tradition or patriarchy can open up instantly because in the midst of such massive disruption, innovation becomes essential not only to surviving, but to thriving.

> ## EXERCISE
>
> Stop for a minute and ask yourself: How has the pandemic experience been for me? Take a moment now that we are on the cusp of a new beginning to record three to five learnings from the time of COVID-19. Jot down the first insights that come to you without overthinking it.
>
> Next, take a moment to honor yourself for doing what you needed to do each and every day to keep yourself, your family, your friends, your colleagues, your neighbors, and your child's school community going while also continuing the work for racial and gender justice. Jot those things down too.
>
> Tuck them away where you can find them later, preferably writing them in the accompanying workbook I've provided, which can be downloaded from www.intentioningbook.com. I predict that our reflections will prompt us to also think about the things we wish we had done during this time. Some of these may even become part of your intentioning practice going forward.

The 21st-Century Challenge

Before the pandemic, progress toward leadership parity for women and people of color was already maddeningly slow. Sometimes it felt like watching paint dry for those of us who have been working to achieve full equality in pay and leadership for years. When I take the long view, however, I can see the immense progress that has been made. The twentieth century was all about opening doors through changing laws and seeing female firsts push through many glass ceilings. The challenge of the twenty-first century is to walk with high intention through those doors that have been opened.

The pandemic has exacerbated disparities to be sure. It's been predicted that women's progress will be set back by at least a decade, due to the combination of job loss and caregiving responsibilities that women shoulder disproportionately. This is especially true as it applies to childcare.[4]

During times of economic disruption, it is women who are more likely than male partners to assume the role of caregiver for family members both in the generations preceding and following them. Mental health in the wake of COVID is consequently at what experts are calling "crisis level." According to a plethora of reports, women are experiencing what is being dubbed a "shecession," with female unemployment at its highest since 1948 and job loss occurring disproportionately among Black, Indigenous, and Latinx women.[5] The Brookings Institute points out that before COVID, women of all races, but again disproportionately women of color, were already overrepresented in low-paying jobs, with 37 percent of men in low-paying jobs compared to 47 percent of women.[6]

Yet as grim as this reality sounds, we are now in a moment ripe with opportunities to mobilize and effect wholesale and lasting change. The national attention is finally focused on racial and gender justice. The fact that the two are inextricably intertwined, as we will discuss further in chapter 4, is also becoming increasingly evident. As I said earlier, massive disruptions always open the door to new thinking and innovation, and thus, in my mind, to optimism and action. It is also an opening to rethink caregiving in general, and childcare in particular, as many other countries have done by regarding caregiving as necessary infrastructure and a social good instead of a burden to be borne disproportionately by women.

That is why providing you with intentioning as a mindset and with very specific Leadership Intentioning Tools, enabling you to create the lives and livelihoods you want, have become so vitally important. Why reading this book is such a tremendously crucial first step for you to take. And why that wonderful line from a movie I have forever loved keeps resonating: "You always had the power, my dear. You just had to learn it for yourself." We must do more than click our heels to get home to our true selves, though. We must learn to embrace the awesome power of our intentions and we must do it now.

....

CHAPTER 2

WHAT DOES SEX HAVE TO DO WITH IT?

Let me, for a moment, address the subtitle of this book: *Sex, Power, Pandemics, and How Women Will Take the Lead for (Everyone's) Good*. One word in particular may have you scratching your head. "What does "sex" have to do with it?" you might ask. And to that I say, "Only everything—starting with culturally defined and assigned gender roles and extending to whomever then holds power from the bedroom to the boardroom." That women have a different view of power than men is key.

How do I know this? Well, my previous bestselling book: *No Excuses: 9 Ways Women Can Change How We Think About Power* deeply explores women's relationships with power. Through that book's own set of actionable tools, women are provided with a framework that transforms power from its oppressive form, encountered as "power *over*," to its generative form, best expressed as "power to."

....

Based on that power transformation, women are able to thrive in the world of work as it is, while also changing it.

....

Here's where I give you the "CliffsNotes" version of my earlier book and the research that informed my conclusion that women's culturally learned ambivalent relationships with power must be and can be transformed into a positive one in order to reach parity in power, position, and pay. This fundamental concept is the theoretical basis for you to understand women and power and will help you break through to higher intentions for yourself and your career. (If you want to take a deeper dive with many up-to-date resources, you can take my online self-study course, "9 Leadership Power Tools to Accelerate Your Career" at the following link, https://courses.taketheleadwomen.com/onlinecourse.)

Here's the Backstory on Writing *No Excuses* and Coming to Its Conclusions

Remember that moment in 2008 when it seemed as if the U.S. might elect its first female president the first time? *ELLE* magazine invited me to write an article on women running for office. What a positive topic I thought, except that I quickly discovered women *weren't* running.[7] At the time, they were half as likely as men to even consider it. And equally important, when they did run, they rarely did so because of their own desires to hold a position of power; they ran to solve a problem, rectify an injustice, or because someone asked them. Actually, they had to be asked *several* times in almost all cases.

The U.S. Congress was only 18 percent female then—and guess what: you can't win if you don't run. I quickly discovered that this reluctance wasn't exclusive to public office; it applied to women and top leadership positions across all industries too. It was the same dynamics and the same 18 percent everywhere. And the pay gap stood persistently at around 20 percent on average, and much greater then, as now, for women of color.

I was astounded. I'd spent decades working to shatter glass ceilings. My first political contribution was in 1972 for the Equal Rights Amendment (ERA), a proposed amendment to the United States Constitution to guarantee equal legal rights for all

American citizens regardless of sex. It calls for an end to distinctions between men and women in terms of divorce, property, employment, and other matters. Most people don't know that aside from the 19th Amendment expressly stating that a U.S. citizen could not be prevented from voting on the basis of their sex, women are completely ignored in the U.S. Constitution. This omission gave tacit permission for hundreds of state and federal restrictions on women's rights to exist and allowed discriminatory hiring practices, including the regular publication of "help wanted, male only" ads and disqualifying women from certain jobs due to perceived weaknesses—physical, intellectual, or emotional.

As mentioned, the year 2020 marked the 100th anniversary of the 19th Amendment. But Indigenous women didn't get voting rights until 1924; restrictions on Asian-Americans' voting rights weren't fully lifted until the 1950s; and the voting rights of Black women and Black men lacked protection under the law until the Voting Rights Act of 1965. Currently, attempts to suppress Black and Brown voters' rights are rearing their ugly heads in a number of states by the closing of polling places, the purging of voter rolls, and the reemergence of restrictive voter ID laws.

Dr. Martin Luther King Jr.'s observation that, "The arc of the moral universe is long but it bends toward justice" may be true, but the question remains, just how long must that arc be? I want to bend it much faster through intentioning.

In 2008, when I researched and wrote that *ELLE* article on women and political office, I had to come to terms with the discomforting fact that women's rights advocates such as myself had opened doors and changed many laws, but our sisters were still stuck, occupying less than 20 percent of top leadership positions across all sectors despite besting men in education. They had been earning 57 percent of college degrees for two decades, which prepared them well enough to assume any role they chose.[0] Despite constituting half of the workforce. Despite demonstrating beyond a shadow of a doubt that companies with more women in leadership roles are more profitable. Furthermore, women held the power of the purse, as at that time they were the decision-makers for 85 percent of consumer purchases.

I wanted to know *why, despite the fact that women ostensibly already had the power they needed,* this leadership disparity continued. That question led me to spend the next two years delving into research, interviewing women across the country, and examining my own patterns of giving away my power. Even though I'd been fortunate in my career to rise from the grassroots to positions interacting with those in the highest halls of power, I discovered I still had to confront my own power demons.

I realized that while many overt and subtle systemic barriers and biases remained, they were no longer the biggest impediment to gender parity in leadership. I had to come face-to-face with the hard truth that women have been socialized differently from men regarding power and therefore, around intention. That reality has deterred us from embracing our phenomenal power and walking with bold intention through the doors we have propped open.

As author Sally Kempton admonished in her book *Before It's Too Late: Helping Women in Controlling or Abusive Relationships,* "It's hard to fight an enemy who has outposts in your head."

I came to understand that the enemy in our head, the messages from media, culture, and perhaps even parents, reward us for staying small physically and for playing small, too, rather than for taking big risks with the inherent possibility of losing big. I also realized that until women achieve equal pay, power, and positions, we will keep fighting the same battles for fairness and equity over and over. I couldn't bear that.

· ·

We had to change the paradigm, embrace our power, and elevate our

intentions to lead if we were ever to breakthrough to leadership parity.

Because let's face it—power unused is power useless.

· ·

So sparked by the inquiry for that piece in *ELLE*, I wrote my fourth book, *No Excuses: 9 Ways Women Can Change How We Think About Power.*[9] My aim was to uncover why these disparities continue, and being a practical activist, to offer some solutions or "Leadership Power Tools" in each chapter that would help women on their journeys. After it was published, I found that I had unwittingly written a powerful leadership book rather than a social commentary alone. People asked me to deliver workshops for women at various career stages, and I saw the results: significant breakthroughs in leadership advancement and compensation, regardless of profession or sector. I realized that I could certainly reach people through these solo efforts, but to make the quantum change necessary for women to ascend to true parity in power, position, and pay, it was essential that I form an organization and a movement. And so, Take The Lead was born and with it some guiding principles.

If you take away only one thing from this synopsis, let it be these core concepts for your power transformation:

• •

Power unused is power useless. Power *over* is oppression. Power *to* is leadership.

A leader is someone who gets stuff done. For that, she needs her Power Tools.

• •

I discovered we must always start with transforming power if we are to free ourselves to embrace our phenomenal power with, as I've come to say repeatedly like a mantra, "confidence, authenticity, and joy." This enables us to bring the locus of power inside of ourselves rather than respond primarily to external forces, such as what others think of us. Then and only then can we elevate our intention to become all we are capable of being. This turned out to be the missing element in all the women's leadership programs I studied. No wonder they were hardly moving the dial.

If that sounds radical to you, you are right. Yet it is also radically simple: It recognizes that power has no attributes of its own.

It's like a hammer. You can build something with it or use it to break something apart. *You* define what it is; nothing about it is hardwired. And how we define, perceive, and activate power is entirely culturally learned.

··

All struggles for equality and justice are fundamentally about power. But the traditional narratives about power are dysfunctional. They are rooted in wars and fighting over resources that are perceived to be finite.

··

That's why the transformation of how we define power, how we know our own power, and how we use power is as fundamental to achieving the goals of leadership gender parity as it is to our individual ability to have the career and life of our dreams.

The power paradigm shift from power *over* to power **to** is at the heart of it. Before we can fully set about intentioning at our highest and best vibration, we must deconstruct the power paradigm as we have been socialized to know it and transform power as a concept.

I am encouraged to see that so many women have stepped up to run for public office in 2018 and 2020. Many ran for exactly the reasons stated earlier: to solve a problem, rectify an injustice, or because someone—likely other women—coaxed them. You may well be the person to join them. The person who will provide the leadership that the world needs now—positive, inclusive, and empathetic leadership that embraces the power **to** model, and that underlies the entire context and curriculum of *Intentioning*. Perhaps this is the moment when together, we can lead from the power **to** create more justice and more abundance instead of leading from fear—whether fear of losing privilege or fear of losing our lives. We can change the narrative and show the world that there is no finite pie, and that when we help each other, we all can have more.

We need a wholesome rebalancing and resetting of the power paradigm. We need to move from the old oppressive, power *over* model where whoever has the strongest army or the most money can control everyone else, to the power *to* model where generative, creative, innovative ideas, energy, and action prevail. This is how we make the world a better place for everyone—a place where technology solutions, healing health care, and well-conceived, well-funded caregiving occurs. Where society's soul evolves because of movements such as #BlackLivesMatter, #metoo, and dare I say, #taketheleadwomen.

••••••••••••••••••••••••••••••

There are still no excuses not to do this.

••••••••••••••••••••••••••••••

As Beyoncé said, *"It's time for women to step up and take the lead."* And Beyoncé is always right.

But as my neighbor Mary Lee used to say when we were struggling young mothers in West Texas, "We have to start where we are, not where we wish we were."

To hearken back to the wisdom Glinda shared with Dorothy, "Home is a place we all must find, my child. It's not just a place where you eat or sleep. Home is knowing. Knowing your mind, knowing your heart, knowing your courage. If we know ourselves, we're always home, anywhere." Substitute "intentioning" for "knowing" and there you are. For as Dorothy concluded after searching everywhere for her power, "If I ever go looking for my heart's desire again, I shouldn't look any farther than my own backyard."

Again, as you look in your own "yard," so to speak, contemplate the question, "the power to do *what?*" The answer will present itself as you will soon see in the Lead Like a Woman framework, the Leadership Intentioning Tools, and stories of the many intentioning women you will meet in this book.

CHAPTER 3

....

THREE WOMEN, THREE INTENTIONING STRATEGIES FOR DISRUPTIVE TIMES

Contrary to prevailing (biased) wisdom, women are actually good at math. We know there can be more than one path to solving a problem. The equation 6+3=9 but so does 5+4 and 7+2. I interviewed many women while writing this book and was inspired by hearing about their varied and significant intentions. It seemed to me that each of them looked around in her own backyard to get in touch with her heart's true desire, and when she found it, she exercised her power *to* in meaningful but differing ways, including how she dealt with life's inevitable challenges—with or without ruby slippers.

Three of these women responded to pandemic-induced *disruption* in ways that represent three strategies. You'll get to know each of them more fully in subsequent chapters, but for now, this brief introduction to their stories will give you insights to help you trust in your own instincts and power *to* intentions, regardless of what pebbles or mountains try to trip you up.

Heli Rodriguez Prilliman was well into making her bold intention come true. Hailing from a small town in Texas (I relate to that), this daughter of a Mexican immigrant father and Mexican-American mother set out with a plan to revolutionize the $20B nail salon industry. She had created new technology that was safer both for nail technicians and clients, an online training program for prospective technicians and salon owners, and a new business model that would enable them to build their own salons and earn livable wages. Her kinetic Instagram stories chronicled her start-up life, including the challenges and successes she faced as a kick-ass feminist female of color determined to turn her vision into a multibillion-dollar concern called Lacquerbar. She had secured investors to finance her enterprise and was ready to lift off.

Then, *boom*, that mountain appeared to block her path. Let's take a trip back to exactly what it felt like in that moment when COVID-19 reared its submicroscopic head.

By mid-March 2020, as the U.S. began to close down, nail salons were among the first to suffer. California, where Heli is headquartered, was one of the hardest hit locations, trending deep burgundy on the daily maps that report the prevalence of COVID-19. It's hard to conjure a business that could be more swiftly devastated by a disease spread through direct human contact than nail salons. When I conducted my interview with Heli, she was at the apex of her over-the-rainbow intentioning. I was so impressed with her courage and, well, her intention. Building a nail tech empire that empowers other women to build their businesses in the same field is definitely a power *to* endeavor. But Heli's business and industry, like so many others, was on hold until the CDC and state and local governments issued the go-ahead for reopening. That, in turn, made it even more difficult to raise the investment funding she had been on the road to getting before the pandemic. According to Crunchbase, female-founded companies received a paltry 3.4 percent of venture capital dollars in 2019. In 2020, that declined even more, to 2.4 percent.[10]

Heli chose to **reset**. She created an online course and provided it free to nail techs to prepare them with her techniques for the time they could reopen, as many have by now. As of this writing, the neon sign in her still shuttered Berkeley salon says, "*Nevertheless She Persisted.*" Recognizing that a bend in the road is not an end in the road is all part of intentioning.

On the other end of the spectrum is Tiffany Dufu whose business, The Cru, was a natural for explosive expansion precisely because of the pandemic. The Cru is a peer-coaching service that curates women's support circles. Members of the group help spur one another's professional growth. What started as a location-based, in-person model quickly pivoted to virtual circles. This gave a greater capability to match women with common interests. Boundaries of geography that had limited expansion in the past evaporated overnight. Tiffany likens the enormous opportunity the pandemic brought her to drinking from a firehose. But the point is, she saw the opportunity, seized it, ran with it, and leveraged it. The rapid growth with almost infinite potential has brought The Cru $2 million in investments in the last year[11] and membership just crossed the 1,000 mark. That might have happened absent the pandemic, but there is no denying that the resulting disruption opened people's minds to virtual networking and using such technologies as Zoom, which, in turn, enabled rapid change in her business to occur. For Tiffany the operative word in response to disruption was **retool.**

Somewhere in between the forced pause in Heli's business (during which time she also had a baby!) and the seize-the-moment make-over Tiffany's business underwent, concert pianist Marina Arsenijevic became the archetype of the intentional woman. Her response to the pandemic was to **reimagine** her career. She became so productive it was as if her creativity was on steroids.

The entertainment industry, like so many others, was a highly disrupted sector with live performance venues expected to remain shuttered through the end of 2021, and many closing forever. Overall, entertainment revenues dropped by at least 25 percent.[12]

Yet Marina had never been more active, releasing new music as well as fresh renditions of old favorites. With her concert schedule cancelled, she experimented with many genres and styles as well as rhythms and themes from different cultures. She grew her social media following exponentially by posting high-quality, short video performances daily. She even turned her home into a performance studio where she and her "best friend" (aka, her piano) could easily take center stage. She partnered with operatic tenor John Riesen to further expand her repertoire and reach.

All this activity brought increased global media coverage. In addition to all of this talent and ingenuity, Marina is drop-dead gorgeous and has an equally sparkling personality, assets that, combined with her growing following, have enabled her to become an influencer for brands, adding another aspect to her business.

So there you have it: three different women, three different responses to disruption. Whether resetting, retooling, or reimagining their businesses, these women have shown that there are so many ways that intentioning can work even in the midst of challenges—and certainly now in the aftermath of disruption.

Whatever path you might have taken during this time or are looking to take in the next year, some elements are universal.

For many, the pandemic has brought a sense of despair and derailment. I'm guessing all of us have felt these emotions at some point, whether from contracting the disease, or from losing a loved one, a job, or a sense of control over our lives. For others, COVID-19 has crystallized a larger sense of purpose. What that purpose is varies and depends on who among the 8 or so billion people on the planet you ask.

· ·

What is apparent throughout it all, however, is that humans are infinitely adaptable and the power of intentioning can put you in charge of your life's choices rather than being determined by external forces.

· ·

What might have started with basic bread baking in the earliest days of lockdown has risen into yeasty thinking about alternative futures.

The three strategies illustrating individual women's reactions to disruption also apply to organizational and business strategies overall. And in this moment, the intersection of gender and racial justice leading to equity and parity in leadership are front and center.

Companies are becoming increasingly pressured by the public and their own employees to walk the talk. To live up to the messaging about diversity, equity, and inclusion (DEI) they've posted on their websites and have written into their diversity and inclusion policies for the past several years. This, of course, included advancing women's leadership.

What intentions will you encourage your employer to pursue? What intentions will you pursue without them if they are slow to act? And what intentions will you initiate if you are a business owner yourself? How should organizations of all kinds take this opportunity of disruption to foster a culture of inclusion that will have a positive impact on the bottom line and allow all employees to thrive?

CHAPTER 4

· · · · · · · · · · · · · · · · ·

CREATING A CULTURE
OF INCLUSION

The actress Danai Gurira was quoted in *Bustle* as saying *"I think that a powerful woman of today has to be subversive, because what is conventional is not acceptable for us anymore."*[13] She was reflecting on what all women can learn from her badass character Okoye in the blockbuster film *Black Panther*, and how important it is to eschew the expectations so long placed on us with regard to strength versus femininity.

This observation comes, not surprisingly, from a Black woman who, in addition to her race and gender intersectionality, also has experience living across cultures and countries and speaks multiple languages.[14]

Such cross-cultural identities and experiences, even those that involve the possibility of discrimination and negative implicit biases against us, tend to create superpowers in women that help us navigate effectively to achieve our highest intentionings.

If that sounds counterintuitive, let's talk about it. I contend that racism and sexism are joined at the head and only together can we successfully combat either of them in the quest for leadership parity and equality of opportunity for women and underrepresented groups. I'd go so far as to say that racial and gender justice must go forward together, or they won't go forward at all.

That's because both racism and sexism are rooted in anger stemming from fear about perceived loss of power, perhaps devolving into perceived social slights. That translates into fear of "the other." The focus is then placed on divisions among people. Diversity is bad in their view. And power is seen as a zero-sum game, requiring power *over* others, instead of the expansive power *to* uplift us all. Rather than welcoming a more just and inclusive society, home front, and workplace, people who fear losing power and believe in the "scarce resource, finite pie" way of seeing the world, feel they are losing primacy and privilege. For example, research correlates hatred of women with mass shooters more consistently than any other characteristic, and that hatred is rooted in the fear of losing whatever privilege the perpetrator feels he has had.[15]

When I heard the terrible news of the murders of eight people, six of them Asian women, in Atlanta massage parlors in March 2021, the words of the song from Rodgers and Hammerstein's 1949 musical *South Pacific* kept repeating in my mind:

> *"You've got to be taught*
> *To hate and fear,*
> *You've got to be taught*
> *From year to year,*
> *It's got to be drummed*
> *In your dear little ear*
> *You've got to be carefully taught."*

The song was specifically addressing the anti-Asian prejudice and opposition to interracial marriage that was prevalent at the time the musical premiered. It was no accident that two grandsons of Jewish immigrants to America with experience of oppression in their DNA not only wrote the song but insisted that it be kept in the show when pressure to remove it mounted because it was deemed too controversial. The song was called "communist" and a "threat to American way of life."[16] Meaning, of course, a threat to white male hegemony.

All in all, the Atlanta rampage occurred in the toxic intersection of racism, sexism, poverty, and anti-immigrant screed exacerbated by leaders who blame the coronavirus on China and was laced with mental illness and access to guns. While the focus has been on anti-Asian hatred, it is critical to highlight that the Atlanta killer said straight out he was trying to eradicate his sex addiction. His was a hate crime directed against women who happened to be Asian. And they happened to be Asian because of the particular sexualization and objectification of Asian women.

The sexualization and objectification of women in general could be the subject of another book entirely, and the long-overdue #MeToo resistance movement is rightly a driving force to change the culture around how women's bodies and women's rights to bodily integrity are treated. What used to be the norm when I was a young woman—basically smiling and ducking when a man tried to touch me inappropriately or leered at me in a way that made me uncomfortable—is behavior that young women today know is wrong and are much more empowered to call out as such.

One of the main ways that women have traditionally been kept in a subservient or second-class social position is to deny them the power over their own bodies. And where white women might have been put onto a pedestal or into a gilded cage as a ruse to "protect" them, women of color had no such shield from sexual objectification and harassment. Still, both the pedestal and the assigned lowly status are mirror image ways to keep women "in their place," and that place was certainly not in the executive suite.

High Ideals but Low Reality

Americans rightly pride ourselves on the founding principles of equality, liberty, and justice for all. Yet Black enslavement and genocide of Indigenous people are equally part of our founding history. Laws singling out Asians, Latinx, and various immigrants for discrimination are embedded in our history.

And women? Our equal rights are still not guaranteed. We have yet to include an Equal Rights Amendment in the U.S. Constitution, which until 1920 didn't even recognize women as citizens. Despite having been ratified by the required 38 states, the ERA was declared dead after a nearly 50-year fight in a January 6, 2020, opinion written by the Department of Justice's Office of Legal Counsel under Attorney General William Barr. It was contended that the proposed amendment's time limit had expired. As the validity of this response is being debated in Washington, D.C., at the time of this writing, and legislation aiming to remove the deadline is under consideration, it remains to be seen whether the ERA will take its place as the 28th Amendment to the Constitution soon or whether the battle will have to be fought all over again. For up-to-date information, go to the ERA Coalition website.

What's more, the pay gap still averages 82 cents to a man's dollar, with women of color earning considerably less.[17] Black women earn 63 cents to a man's dollar, AAPI women 85 cents, Latinas 55 cents, and Native American women 60 cents. And, no, this isn't about choices of professions; the numbers are matched for jobs held by full time, year-round workers. As I've noted, I cofounded Take The Lead seven years ago when I saw the meta-data that American women held a paltry 18 percent[18] of the top leadership positions across all sectors then, and though we are now inching toward 25 percent, that is still just half of where we should be to have full equity and equality. After all, equity and equality are what we need for full "R-E-S-P-E-C-T," as the great Aretha Franklin sang.

••

As we intention our way forward, let's face it: some things, like the racial and

gender disparities and injustices that have been laid bare, should never be

normalized again. This is a crystalline example of the opportunity we now have to

create and normalize a much better future. Let's take it, full speed ahead.

••

Given that the coronavirus pandemic, matched by the racism pandemic, has intensified the long-overdue awareness of the urgent call for racial justice, these pandemics have opened minds further to the need for equality among *all* citizens regardless of gender, race, ethnicity, ability, or sexual orientation. The pandemic's disruption has exposed gaping cracks in our social, political, and economic systems. We must seize the moment to normalize new and better opportunities for everyone.

The most pervasive of those inequities has historically been discrimination against women inclusive of every other identifying factor. This exists in virtually every country in the world regardless of its racial makeup and affects 51 percent of the population. We see glimmers of how gender parity can become the prevailing culture in the Scandinavian countries and in a few other countries such as Iceland, which has closed 88 percent of its gender gap, according to the World Economic Forum. The U.S. ranks 53rd among the world's 195 nations.[19]

••

But gender-based discrimination is always crosshatched, or intersected, with

all other aspects of identity, such as race. That's intersectionality.

••

Intersectionality is a term coined by Law Professor Kimberlé Williams Crenshaw.[20] It was first intended to inform legal interpretations of discrimination and was later applied more broadly in the culture. It acknowledges, for example, that Black women experience discrimination and implicit biases differently from white women. It's this complexity that makes it so hard for society—and often women ourselves—to call out discrimination boldly and consistently, in one unified voice, let alone to eliminate it.

••

We must recognize overlapping intersectional identities and experiences and love them all to shape a culture of inclusion.

••••••••••••••••••••••••••••••••••••••

Intersectionality, in the cultural sense, is the recognition that most individuals have many identities and experiences: race, class, gender, age, sexual orientation, religion, ability, and immigration status, among others. As identities overlap, they can compound. Thus a 25-year-old Black Muslim woman may experience gender discrimination differently than a 50-year-old Black Christian woman, or a white woman in either of those religious denominations and ages. This level of holistic inclusion allows individuals to showcase multiple sides and present their whole selves to the world. You can start making space for intersectionality by avoiding oversimplified language.

For myself, I enjoy being a woman, being a Texan/Arizonan/New Yorker, rural/small town/city resident, and being Jewish from the southern U.S. where I experienced almost every mainstream Christian denomination and have had the opportunity to immerse myself in varied cultures, in particular Black and Mexican-American.

Identifying myself this way does not make me less me; it actually enriches me. It expands my consciousness about my own culture and my appreciation for others. It's why I desire to live in a diverse, inclusive community and work in a diverse, inclusive organization.

To be sure, it's easy for any of us to lose track of our own multiple identities, let alone to remain cognizant of other people's.

I recently listened to singer/songwriter Alicia Keys's memoir, *More Myself,* on audio. In it, she reveals much about her identity as a Black person and a woman. But only toward the end of the memoir, when challenged by her husband, Swizz Beats, did she talk specifically about the part of her identity that comes from her mother who raised her and was of Italian heritage. . We make choices, not always conscious ones, about which of our identities and intersectionalities most profoundly define us. But all of our identities represent balances or imbalances of power within the larger culture.

> I invite you to take an intentioning journey with me to rectify the imbalances in our culture for good—meaning "everyone's good" and good as in "forever." To do so we must put all women, in all our diversities and intersectionalities, at the center of the recovery from the pandemic and then onward from there to full social and economic parity.

We've already seen that women have been disproportionately doing the frontline work during the pandemic. One in three jobs held by women has been designated as essential. The headline in *The New York Times*, "How Millions of Women Became the Most Essential Workers in America," frames the situation well.[21] But what the tiny coronavirus also exposed was the full impact of the massive gender imbalance in upper leadership positions regardless of industries. It's men who are disproportionately in the leadership roles. The observation I made as a young woman—that women by and large do the frontline work while the men are in charge—remains a chief factor in gender disparities of all kinds, continuously reinforcing the structural disparities in power and pay.

The authors of that *New York Times* article, Campbell Robertson and Robert Gebeloff, note, "From the cashier to the emergency room nurse to the drugstore pharmacist to the home health aide taking the bus to check on her older client, the soldier on the front lines of the current national emergency is most likely a woman." They then cite several examples that reveal a consistent pattern across various industries, the health care industry being one with the most obvious imbalance. "While women have steadily increased their share of high-end health care jobs like surgeons and other physicians, they have also been filling the unseen jobs proliferating on the lowest end of the wage scale, the workers who spend long and little-rewarded days bathing, feeding and medicating some of the most vulnerable people in the country. Of the 5.8 million people working health care jobs that pay less than $30,000 a year, half are nonwhite, and 83 percent are women."

A pandemic has the power to unravel our livelihoods, upset our lifestyles, and generally turn our lives inside-out . . . swiftly. At the same time, a mass reset is happening in how we work and live. Quite frankly, that reset should include graduating the women who have supported everyone through this crisis to the next level and higher!

If you were among the majority of humans on Earth personally affected in some way by the pandemic, it would be understandable if you missed the news about the abnormally large sandstorm that spread 5,000 miles across the Atlantic, the locusts and jellyfish that appeared as big as dinner plates, the lions that napped on a major road during human lockdown, or the "Great Conjunction" of Saturn and Jupiter that was visible in the winter solstice sky. But even if you haven't heard of any of these newsworthy events, you've almost certainly heard the name of George Floyd. The murder of this unarmed Black man at the hands of a white officer, Derrick Chauvin, while begging for his mother and a breath of air, touched off protests against systemic racism and police brutality across the United States and around the world—for weeks nonstop. Most of the world heaved a collective sigh of relief when Chauvin was convicted and taken off to prison. Even though we know that won't be the end of the story, for Chauvin is already seeking a retrial, it gives us a sense that with superhuman effort, it is at least possible for abuse of state power to be confronted successfully.

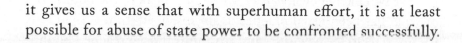

Just as with many other examples of courageous boundary breakers, #BlackLivesMatter was founded by three women.

Alicia Garza, Patrisse Cullors, and Opal Tometi had experienced multiple oppressions from being Black, female, and queer. Founded in 2013, the movement was ripe and ready to ratchet up its particular feminist and inclusive brand of organizing for change by the time the events of 2020 occurred.

Most of the high-profile stories the news media brought forward were about police brutality against Black men and boys to be sure. As news stories go, we are less likely to hear about the women, but horrific offenses against them have been perpetrated as well. Now we know of Breonna Taylor, Tanisha Anderson, and many more. In a pattern replicated throughout our culture, Black women's lives seem to matter less than others, spawning the hashtag #sayhername, along with an intentional effort to include both genders in this conversation. It will have to be intentional because just as women's plight has not had the prominence it deserves in the movement to end police brutality, it will require intentioning to ensure that women are not left out of DEI frameworks and programs.

The convergence of these two pandemics, COVID-19 and racial injustice, is so earthshaking that its aftershocks are going to be felt for years to come.

And therein lies our opportunity.

We will likely never, *never* have such a break in the boundaries of what has been usual practice again in our lifetimes. Therefore, it's up to us to let new thinking rush into those breached boundaries and become accepted practice now. I say this with such emphasis because cultures are famously hard to change—until they do, and then suddenly everyone accepts the new status quo as though it has always been.

Policies within law enforcement are being subjected to investigation and change. Historical monuments with racist roots have been removed. Bands and sports teams have changed their offending names. So many Black women have become mayors of major cities that you can call it a trend. Atlanta Mayor Keisha Bottoms observes that Black women voters are the backbone of the Democratic Party and that it is key to acknowledge both identities, their race and gender, in the push for a more inclusive society. She further notes that she has been subjected to scrutiny that is rarely directed toward men, including speculation over whether she would be able to lead as "her own person."[22]

The iconic photo of Civil Rights hero Congressman John Lewis standing, masked and supported by a cane shortly before his death, alongside Washington, D.C.'s Mayor Muriel Bowser on the Black Lives Matter mural painted boldly near the White House, is seared into my soul.[23]

I was jolted by the death of Lewis, the last living speaker of the 1963 March on Washington,[24] and the stark reminder of how far we have yet to go to achieve racial equality in this country. For me, there has never been a separation between racial and gender justice because I know that all of these identity-based injustices are bound together by systemic privilege, rooted in the white male hegemony that underlies our culture. And Bowser's leadership in many ways represents the next, more gender inclusive generation of the movement.

Racism and sexism are always joined at the top along with homophobia and other tools of a patriarchal power structure designed to create "otherness" that keeps one group privileged while keeping those considered "other" in their place.

Thank you, pandemics, for shaking the boundaries that have sustained these pervasive means of discrimination. But now it is up to us to take the energy of that shakeup and do some serious intentioning with it to advance equality. Appreciation of racial and gender diversity in the culture is an essential first step.

••

Beware the diversity divide. When these two words clash, so do the worlds they represent.

••

Both "diversity" and "divide" start with the prefix "di," meaning "two," "twice," or "double" in most dictionary definitions. But it also can mean "split" or "separate." The leadership challenge is to bridge that split.

A divide can only be resolved by a more intentionally inclusive culture. It requires examples set from the top and systems that enable and value the rich exchange of ideas and innovations that diversity can bring.

The flip side of the diversity divide can be seen in *The New York Times* article entitled, "What Makes an American?"[25] It profiles an immigrant Filipino family finding their way into American culture in Texas. The article celebrates these people for trying to make life better for their loved ones, while also celebrating the fact that the power of assimilation remains strong in the U.S. Through hard work, this family was able to accomplish in a few short years what used to take decades for immigrants to achieve. A nursing job helped pave the way to having a house in the suburbs and an emphasis on education meant the children ultimately made honor roll at school. But the transition for the kids was initially quite difficult as they were aware of their differences.

I relate to this story because all four of my grandparents were immigrants from Eastern Europe who settled in small Texas towns two generations ago. I was reminded in all sorts of ways that my family and I were "other" just like this family. Aside from my grandparents' accents, which I was asked about frequently, we were among the few and sometimes only Jewish families in town. My grandparents had escaped oppression and wanted their children and grandchildren to grow up in the bright light of America's freedom—to look, speak, and act like the predominant culture. Yet I lived in dread of that inevitable moment when someone would ask me, "What church do you go to?" It is typically the first question asked of a new acquaintance in the South.

Our noisy multigenerational house wasn't like the seemingly cheerful *Leave It to Beaver* nuclear family households of my peers. Another difference. How embarrassing. Their mothers didn't work outside the home, whereas mine went to work with my father every day. She wasn't home baking chocolate chip cookies for us after school in a starched apron she had ironed herself. Instead, my grandmother would make her European fried dough cookies with powdered sugar, which she served to my friends, not in a starched apron but in her old blue gingham housedress while wearing no shoes! Although my friends loved those fried dough cookies, I was mortified that the sights and smells in our kitchen were so different. Throughout my childhood and teen years, I wanted nothing more than to fit in, to be like everyone else.

Diversity, in that sense, was a divide for me. The explicit and implicit biases I experienced shaped much of my behavior even as I grew older. My response was to "cover" by taking on the habits of those around me and downplaying the very things that made me who I authentically am.

> **I, too, had covered, just as many women and underrepresented groups in the workforce cover themselves every day.[26]**

By and large, all of us are working in institutions designed by white men for white men who had women, and perhaps people of color, at home taking care of the rest of their lives.

But as I matured, the experience of living in more than one culture made me value diversity rather than fear it. It made me appreciate the many different languages, accents, foods, and habits I encountered growing up. I began to feel as if I had the good fortune of belonging to many tribes. Because I could move among them comfortably, I often felt like a world traveler.

The fact is that I have always loved the richness of human diversity, except for the pain when I was called out as the outlier. So I came to value the experience of being "othered." It gave me empathy for all groups that are marginalized or discriminated against. More importantly, it made me an activist for social justice because I realized that even as we value our uniqueness, we—meaning the human race—will either succeed or fail together in today's interconnected world.

People who don't lead diverse lives nor live in intersecting identities might not value diversity and may instead see it as a divide. We can't escape the reality that, if as a culture we see diversity as a plus, it is a plus; and if we see it as a divide, it will divide us with potentially disastrous consequences.

Now is the time to examine the impact of our own individual and collective behaviors with a serious view to whether we want to create and live in a divided or a diverse society. I'm betting on the good will of the majority to embrace diversity, if for no other reason than because we realize we are all "other" in some way.

Ask yourself, where do I have privilege and where do I not? You probably have some of both, as do I. I live in white skin and have been fortunate enough to have a roof over my head, food to eat, and educational opportunities even though I didn't always take advantage of them. I also live with the constant knowledge that at some point someone is going to lob a sexist, ageist, or anti-Semitic epithet my way.

Let us then intentionally work for the policies and culture most likely to support the positive value of our rich varieties of diversity.

Because what sets you apart, it turns out, is actually what gets you ahead. As teenage climate-justice activist Greta Thunberg observed, "And in a world where everyone strives to act, think and look the same, being different is truly something to be proud of. That's why I'm very proud to be autistic."

Diversity is a plus, equity a necessity, and inclusion is the process to achieve the desired culture where each of us can contribute to our highest and best intention.

Valuing differences provides solutions while creating a culture of inclusion, a topic we will explore further in the next chapter.

CHAPTER 5

....

CORPORATE RESPONSIBILITY
AND OPPORTUNITY

So tell me, what did you have for dinner last night? Italian? French? Chinese? Mexican? Soul food? California nouvelle? I've always wondered why, if we have such wide-ranging tastes, we often don't embrace the wide range of humans who introduced these rich food varieties to our land and to our tables.

Of course, the more important question to ask is how do we get to a place where we genuinely embrace and love such diversity? When will we incorporate into our core belief systems a trust that power shared is *not* power diminished, but in fact, power expanded? The more there is, the more there is. If I help you and you help me, we have both been helped to have more. The larger our network of human relationships is on what I call our "power maps," the more likely we will each be to achieve our intentions.

To further this understanding and to help it flourish exponentially, the very next questions become: What should we expect of the organizations where we work? What responsibilities do they have to promote diversity, equity, inclusion, belonging, and any of the other words that define a healthy unified culture? We must always intentionally include gender and women's leadership parity within that rubric for it is too easily left behind in the Diversity, Equity, and Inclusion conversation.

As Emma Lazarus (a young woman) wrote in her poem emblazoned on the Statue of Liberty (that "mighty woman with a torch," please take note), "Give me your tired, your poor, Your huddled masses yearning to breathe free ...."

If you think about it, diversity is what defines America as a nation more than any other. It's our greatest strength. It makes us interesting. Innovative. Resilient.

Americans have issued the invitation to diversity and diversity has built the country. Yet each new wave of immigrants seems to have been disliked and often discriminated against for one reason or another despite their contributions. A large segment of our diverse population came to these shores enslaved and were forced into being an engine for economic growth, as Nikole Hannah-Jones details in "The 1619 Project,"[27] an ongoing initiative from *The New York Times Magazine* that aims to reframe the narrative of American history by placing the consequences of slavery and the contributions of Black Americans at the center of the nation's economic, political, and social story.

And the entire country is built on lands taken violently from the Indigenous peoples by European explorers who, because of their privilege and ethnocentrism, assumed entitlement to do so. The current trend to do land acknowledgments is one attempt to recognize this reality.

Given our checkered past, we have hard issues to deal with before we fully realize the lofty ideals of the Founding Fathers. Not that they lived up to those ideals themselves.

Let us not forget that there were no Founding Mothers. When Abigail Adams beseeched her husband and future president of the United States, John Adams, to "remember the ladies," he responded by laughing at her and asserting that his colleagues then drafting the Constitution of the new nation would not endure such a "tyranny of the petticoat."

Women are still waiting to be remembered via the Equal Rights Amendment to guarantee us full equality under the law, and women's reproductive rights are still under assault. When I held my first CEO position, I was unable to get credit in my own name even though I was earning more than my then-husband. I could not have inherited property in my state, and the "Help Wanted" ads were segregated into "male" and "female" posts.

When we see how much more effectively countries with women leaders have managed COVID, we can speculate that a nation founded and led equally by women and men might come closer to living its highest ideals and have better outcomes in such areas as health care, public safety, and education. And by extension as well as by all existing data, we can expect that companies founded and led equally by men and women will have better economic results.

The data backs up this assumption. Far from being a zero-sum game, diversity, including gender diversity, enriches as it expands knowledge, innovation, and the mental agility to solve complex problems. Still, the value of diversity isn't automatically recognized and is often overlooked because of our implicit biases.

In "The Diversity–Innovation Paradox in Science," published in the *Proceedings of the National Academy of Sciences,* April 2020 edition, researchers Bas Hofstra et al[28] measured scientific innovations, the impact/adoption of those innovations, and career trajectories of U.S. PhD recipients and their dissertations across three decades. They found that underrepresented groups produce higher rates of innovation, but their contributions are devalued and discounted.

Simply stated, diversity in terms of gender, race and ethnicity improves the bottom line. A study conducted by the Boston Consulting Group (BCG) looked at 1,700 companies across 8 different countries of varying sizes within varying industries and found that those with diverse management teams enjoyed as much as 19 percent higher revenue due to their innovative outlook and practices.[29] So it's no surprise that companies today, for the most part, say they value diversity, though they execute it with greater or lesser success depending on several factors.

••

Why do some diversity programs fail? And more importantly,

what can we do differently to achieve success?

•••••••••••••••••••••••••••••••••••••

Many CEOs and professionals in the Diversity, Equity, and Inclusion or Human Resources spaces have been pondering a perplexing question: Why, after so many fine words and so much time and money expended on DEI programs, is it still stubbornly hard to move the dial?

In delving into the problem with them, it's clear that many traditional diversity programs are not only largely ineffective, but in some instances have the opposite effect of increasing implicit and explicit biases. These problems have been exacerbated by the coronavirus pandemic, since, as we have seen, the majority of job losses have been to women, and the majority of those to women of color. But that's all the more reason to do things differently.

For example, the leaky pipeline of female employees in the tech field exists not because there are too few women in STEM or that the potential pool of female employees is inadequate, but rather, because people don't see other people who look like themselves in leadership positions and often feel undervalued by a culture that is built around high-testosterone male-dominated structures. It is therefore incumbent upon a company that has made diversity, equity, and inclusion a stated value to create deliberate ways to advance women and people of color into its leadership at all levels and in true partnership. One Black woman "twofer" as head of DEI cobbled onto a leadership team absent of other diversity does not solve the problem and in fact it may just set her up for failure.

The reasons for lack of successful Diversity, Equity, Inclusion, Belonging programs (or whatever names and acronyms are given to them) are manifold, but they basically boil down to these three:

1. **Lack of commitment from the top**. Absence of support at the highest level of the organization is a sure-fire way to fail at increasing diversity. Even if a CEO vocalizes commitment but believes the organization is a meritocracy, it's quite likely that leadership will continue to look like the CEO; it's human nature to believe those with attributes we share are the most meritorious unless there is willingness to challenge one's own assumptions. And despite the unassailable business case that more gender and diversity of all kinds result in more profits, it's not likely that anyone in the currently largely white and male power structure is going to relinquish their power voluntarily. As a result, BCG managing director Matt Krentz found: "Half of all diverse employees stated that they see bias as part of their day-to-day work experience. Half said that they don't believe their companies have the right mechanisms in place to ensure that major decisions (such as who receives promotions and stretch assignments) are free from bias. By contrast, white heterosexual males, who tend to dominate the leadership ranks, were 13 percentage points more likely to say that the day-to-day experience and major decisions are free of bias."[30]

2. **Focusing on the problem and not the solution**. Instead of courageously having the conversations that can lead to solutions, companies not meeting their DEI goals tend to discuss the data about the lack of diversity and to default to shame and blame. That's a depressing and energy-sucking misuse of time and resources. Moreover, it reinforces a culture where Black, Indigenous, and other people of color, as well as all women, don't see evidence that they will be treated fairly as they work to achieve their career intentions.

3. **Failing to change the culture**. So many companies simply do not create a workplace environment where all feel and actually are valued. Let's face it: It's hard to change a

culture while you are living in it. I'm not saying it's easy. But the primary reason so many women bail out of the corporate world mid-career has much more to do with discomfort in the culture than with the prevailing assumptions that they leave for childbearing reasons. Similarly, the existence of a white supremacist culture within a workplace is often not even recognized as a deterrent, and you can't change what you don't see needs changing.

By contrast, Felicia Davis, founder and CEO of the Black Women's Collective and a Take The Lead Leadership Ambassador, describes Take The Lead's approach of creating a culture of inclusion as follows: "We are tackling DEI from the racial healing perspective and using psychology-based tools so that women and men show up to work with the capacity to have powerful and sometimes polarizing conversations that matter. We do this in order to challenge, transform and confront systemic racism in a way that creates more equitable and inclusive cultures."

"The Culture Is the Weather"

Former Intel Chief Diversity Officer and President of the Intel Foundation Rosalind Hudnell also has a very clear and cogent way of looking at corporate culture. In a powerful keynote speech she gave at a Paradigm for Parity conference I attended, she observed that the organizational culture is the weather within which diversity will thrive if it is fully embraced by leadership and intentionally implemented in practice.

"Strategy is simple," says Hudnell. "Execution is hard." She goes on to observe that most of the challenges in companies today are not related to whom you're biased *against* but rather to whom you are biased *for*. This emanates directly from who has privilege and who doesn't, and whether they value diversity or not. Like the white male CEO with an all-white and almost all-male executive team, who assured me that his company was a meritocracy without realizing that we usually see those most similar to us as most meritorious.

These biases wreak their havoc in ways both obvious and subtle. For example, according to research by Payscale:[31]

[E]mployees who have a white male advocate often end up with higher pay, and most of those employees are white men Women—particularly black and Hispanic women—are the least likely to have such a lucrative connection .... Some 56.7% of all respondents reported having a sponsor at work. Of white male respondents who said they have a sponsor, 90% said their sponsor was white. Among black and Hispanic women who said they have a sponsor, only 60% said their sponsor was white. Another study by the Center for Talent Innovation found that most executives choose protégés who look like them.[32]

∙∙∙

"Leaders who don't lead diverse lives can't adequately

build and lead diverse teams," says Hudnell.

∙∙∙

Though he unfortunately fails to include gender diversity, Ben Hecht, writing in *Harvard Business Review*, does a good job of articulating the power imbalances within organizations that hold them back from embracing diversity by concluding, "Instead of trying to change *some* people to fit the organization, we must focus on transforming our organizations to fit *all* people." And he encourages us to ask, "What informal and formal power do I hold to shift culture? How should I wield it to change damaging norms and power dynamics within our institution?"[33]

Berkshire Hathaway CEO, and one of the wealthiest people in the world, Warren Buffett has observed that he is optimistic about the future precisely because of women. The point he makes is that our country and companies have traditionally been using only half the available brainpower and innovation by discriminating against women. So once the doors are open to full gender parity, we'll double our capabilities.[34]

5 Tips to Make the Workplace Better by Reckoning with Lived Experience

Here are 5 tips that can help you and your organization take advantage of the current emphasis on race, gender, and other diversities, and turn this opportunity for genuine dialogue into a realizable vision for a better future workplace.

1. Avoid the pitfalls of traditional diversity training that can often exacerbate implicit biases by making people of privilege defensive and people from traditionally under-represented groups shut down or feel the effort is merely window dressing.[35]

   From my experience working within organizations, I have come to believe that everyone must be brought into the story to make sustainable change for inclusion. We can help companies create a workplace where everyone is valued for who he, she, or they are and for what they bring to the company's purpose. It's important that people are fully versed in the benefits diversity presents for them. Here are just a few data points to share:

   - Higher ratio of women leaders in upper management = **higher ROI, better decisions**. (Catalyst,[36] McKinsey,[37] EY,[38] Bain,[39] World Bank,[40] and more.[41])
   - **83 percent of millennials** are more actively engaged when they believe their company fosters an inclusive culture. (Deloitte)[42]
   - "Teams that operate in an **inclusive culture** outperform their peers by a staggering **80 percent**." (Deloitte)[43]
   - Gender equality throughout the workforce would add $13 trillion to the global economy. (McKinsey)[44]

2. Make a transparent plan with measurable accountability. Accountability always starts at the top with the CEO, the board, and the executive team. Any intervention that

starts without their buy-in and willingness to show up is destined to fail.

3. Take the opportunity of this disruptive time to incorporate changes that will help women come back into the workforce while creating a long-term shift in norms about how men and women assume family responsibility.

    a. Maximize family leave for caregiving equally for men and women. Are you aware that women are now spending an average of 7.7 more hours per day than men on childcare?[45] This is not preordained but it is clearly one of the reasons why women experience so much workplace stress and as a result are more likely to leave for caregiving responsibilities. Workplace expectations and culture can help to change it.

    b. Make it attractive or mandatory that men take parental leave equal to women. This can be stretched out over a period of time, but experiences in the Nordic countries have shown that not only does this policy help moms, it organically engages dads more with their children from birth. The results of that interaction both for fathers and children are extremely positive.

    c. From the organizational culture perspective, be sure to eliminate bias toward fathers—the "daddy benefit"—that assumes fathers will be better employees because of parental responsibility and toward mothers—the "mommy penalty"—that assumes mothers will be less devoted employees because their attention will be diverted by their children.

    d. Support making quality childcare readily available to all families as essential infrastructure and a social good. While many if not most companies might not be able to provide on-site daycare, there are various other ways that helping subsidize the cost for employees can be done. Not the least of this is by supporting public policies that level the field for families needing child-care regardless of their economic circumstances. There is no better investment than in preschool children, as long-term studies of Head Start have demonstrated.

4. The work-from-home experiences necessitated by the pandemic have taught everyone that flexible work hours and locations without losing productivity are eminently possible. They have allowed the talents of people with disabilities to be incorporated into the workforce seam-lessly. They have enabled women and men to attend to the needs of their families while fulfilling their work duties. Continue to experiment with ways to allow for many individual situations. I can assure you that the competi-tion for female talent isn't coming as much from other companies; it's from women themselves who decide to start their own businesses in order to avoid the corporate world altogether. The bottom line is that flexibility for workers increases their loyalty to a company at the same time as it reduces the stress that might be detracting from productivity or even causing them to leave for other opportunities.

5. Attend to the systems changes that can help prevent unintentional discrimination and alleviate the effects of implicit or unconscious bias. For example, blind resumes with names removed can eliminate the proven bias against women and people of color in the interview process. We have seen that when reviewing resumes from men and women with commensurate experience, the male applicant is often assumed to be more competent and thus is more likely to be hired than the female applicant. Simulations have shown the same is true when considering resumes of applicants with African-American-sounding names. Those candidates are less likely to get a favorable recom-mendation than those with white-American-sounding

names. Sociologist Cordelia Fine does a remarkable job of eviscerating the notions that men and women are simply hardwired differently in her book *Delusions of Gender* and showing in fine detail how implicit biases creep into research that concludes gender differences in proclivities and behaviors are preordained.[46] And these findings apply just as well to assumptions about race.

6. But don't expect systems changes to change hearts and minds. To get to the hearts and minds element, consider taking the Harvard Implicit Bias test.[47] It's an excellent baseline that provides many aha moments, even for people who think they understand implicit bias, and it does so without pointing fingers or assigning blame. Most people want to be fair and to see themselves as in favor of equality. This test will show them where they may be falling short so they can improve and meet their personal goal of being more inclusive.

7. Culture change is a long-lead process. It begins with a strategy and commitment from the executive team, which cascades to training employee leadership, who in turn engage and assist the rest of the company, facilitating purposeful conversations and exercises over a period of time, until the culture sought permeates the company. Such a process can be and has been quite effective for many organizations. As Hudnall said, "Culture is the weather."

Creating a culture of inclusion is a journey, not a sprint. Be sure to set timetables and benchmarks and to celebrate successes. Own up to failures and share what will be done to fix them.

Also be sure to celebrate the diversity of your group and share in all its richness frequently and intentionally. To bring the message back to where I started, a good old-fashioned potluck meal where everyone can talk about their families and the food of their culture or country of origin is a never-fail way to do that.

All of this will create a smoother, less-impeded runway for the women who are intentioning to join the leadership ranks. And in the process, it will construct an entirely new framework for leadership theory and practice going forward.

· · · · · · · · · · · · · · · · ·

CHAPTER 6

LEAD LIKE A WOMAN: FRAMEWORK FOR THE NEW FUTURE

Since I wrote *No Excuses* and have been sharing both the "Power Concepts" that change the power paradigm and the "9 Leadership Power Tools" with thousands of others, I've seen women express a great deal more confidence, authenticity, joy, and above all, *intentioning* in their careers and in their lives. Even those who have left the workforce in exhaustion due to the caregiving burdens of the pandemic are, for the most part, primed to get back to work in one form or another. Maybe it will be by rejoining a company; maybe it will be starting their own companies. But either way, they'll be leading authentically as women. If there is one thing we have learned consciously or unconsciously in the last decades of workforce experience, it's that trying to fit ourselves into a structure that's not designed to include or advance us is never going to be successful.

Imagine for a moment that women had created the institutions we work in. What would be different? What would be the same? The fact that childcare is such a burr-under-the-saddle issue today, when having babies is nothing new in human experience says to me that we definitely need to put women in more leadership roles. I suspect that if women had designed the workplace, we would have figured out long ago how to be productive *and* care for our families simultaneously.

Although change is never one and done, I do see progress despite the setbacks of the pandemic. And there are practical as well as philosophical reasons for this.

More secure income for families is critical but not the only benefit of women rising in the workplace; it has led to other positive changes in who shoulders household duties. I see more power sharing in personal relationships, particularly in the area of childcare. While the pandemic has laid bare the fact that women still bear the brunt of caregiving—not just childcare but also care for the elderly and infirm—it also has propelled more men into their rightful share of caregiving responsibilities, or at least opened their eyes to the need for alternate solutions.

When women embrace their power, they can be their authentic selves. They have less depression and handwringing over their life choices. There's an assumption now that women in the workplace are the norm, not the exception.

And then there is that data I cited previously in chapter 5, a strong business case for women's leadership as well as ethical motivation for a more diverse and inclusive workplace. The pandemic has provided fertile ground to plant seeds of change and to test theories about leadership that would not have previously been questioned.

••

So what do you think? Are women better than men at leading through crisis?

••

I don't know about you, but when I am asked this, my mind immediately goes to all the practice I've had handling my children's spats, injuries, and emergencies real or perceived. I am pretty sure that experience prepared me well to handle what I call crossroads decision moments with a cool head, empathy, and reasonably good judgment in my professional life. I've faced a wide range of challenges from an employee dying of a heart attack at work, to anthrax attacks and firebombs at my office, to 9/11 and its direct impact on thousands of individuals in the organization I led as well as on the city, state, and country as a whole.

We know that female legislators pass more bills and are more likely to work across the aisle to get the people's work done. We know that companies with more women in their leadership make more money. We know that diversity in general makes for better innovation and greater alignment with the marketplace.

Yet no specific leadership behavior is inherently gendered.

Paradoxically the implicit bias and discrimination women have endured has, I believe, acculturated superpowers into our thinking and behavior. I know this is all a bit radical and I will expound on this belief further in Leadership Intentioning Tool #8, Turn Implicit Bias on Its Head and into Your Superpowers, but for now consider that our leadership styles tend to be more acutely aware of the human side of events, as well as the economic factors. We are trained to be multitaskers. We can hold multiple tabs open in our brains while calmly taking care of problems, because that has been our survival mechanism.

The data shows that women tend to be more philanthropic.[48] In a pandemic, that matters. It also matters in a recovery. I watched a conversation with Lynn Good, the female CEO of Duke Energy, and was super impressed with her thoughtful attention to the details of how we bring people back to work safely, rather than pushing the macho envelope to get them back as fast as possible.[49]

It oversimplifies things to say that women are always better leaders in a crisis or at any other time. But in my research, and while delivering training in the resulting curriculum to thousands of women by now, I have found that changing the power paradigm for women elevates their leadership intentions and gives them the tools to thrive in the world as it is while realizing they have the skills and the agency to change it into the world they want it to be.

Of course, the culturally learned assets women bring to leadership also have their flip side: being more tentative in our language and often more risk averse are two such examples. Being thoughtful and getting the facts is good for sure, but leadership always involves having to make choices from imperfect solutions with limited resources and usually less than enough information. So women need to exercise the confidence and courage to take action and own it. The more one exercises those muscles the stronger she gets.

My own challenges through the pandemic have required me to flex my entrepreneurial muscles more than ever. Take The Lead has been an entirely virtual organization populated by independent contractors from the get-go, so nothing has changed about how we work on a daily basis. That said, the pandemic has disrupted everyone's life in some way. We have parents who are now also teachers, entrepreneurs who have lost clients, people whose friends or family have had COVID, and the same general anxiety that washes over the rest of the country. So we began to start every team meeting with a round of questions about how people are doing emotionally as well as physically. We share ways of coping.

At the same time as I acknowledge where we are today, I keep us focused on what's ahead. I made a point to change the framing on an agenda item someone had posted from "Coronavirus response strategy" to "Revenue generating strategy." People tend to be in response mode unless a leader—regardless of gender—helps them focus on an intentional and positive thought process where we create our own opportunities or take advantage of opportunities in front of us.

We are pivoting all of our offerings to virtual ones and growing earned revenue, so we are not always totally dependent on philanthropy. That way we can use philanthropic funds as investments to grow capacity, create new programs, and provide free services to those most in need.

We have the advantage of great leadership training and coaching content that can be expressed and used virtually. We launched a new, improved, online, self-directed "9 Leadership Power Tools to Accelerate Your Career" course with a goal to reach 10,000 women with it. I attribute being in the midst of a pandemic to helping me realize that this course is an incredibly valuable asset that we can offer to companies as a cost-effective way to keep preparing their female talent to move up the leadership pipeline.

We are also partnering with other organizations to leverage our constrained resources. For example, we have conducted virtual workshops with Luminary, the coworking community, and we have held a webinar series on building a better future for women in the legal profession in partnership with the Center for Women in Law. We launched our immersive 50 Women Can Change the World in Journalism on schedule in mid-June 2020 via a virtual format for the first time.[50] We had only half the funding we needed for the program, but I made the decision to proceed anyway because the need was there and the commitment had already been made.

I will use the word "always" in this instance, to say that there is *always* a way to achieve one's mission. Sometimes you have to think very creatively to find the means, but it's always there, often right under your nose, I promise you, if you have the wisdom to see it and the courage to use it.

••

So here are three tips forming a framework to help you use the best of the characteristics that are frequently identified with female leadership so you too can *lead* like a woman. And by the way, men can use these too.

••

1. **Empathy:** Take out a sheet of paper and list all the ways you notice people exhibiting empathy during this

pandemic. Then ask yourself how can you tap into the power of this well of empathy to inspire yourself and the people you work with to come out of the pandemic stronger, more caring, and more prosperous. These are not antithetical characteristics.

2. **Collaboration:** If you work with other people, ask them to do the same empathy exercise independently of you. Then compare notes and look for the nuggets of gold in the wisdom you have collectively amassed. If you work alone, gather several peers to do this exercise with you. Ask if there are opportunities to collaborate profitably or to leverage resources with the ideas that surface.

3. **Strong values, low ego decision-making:** Get comfortable with the idea that there are problems and there are predicaments. Problems have solutions. Predicaments require you to make decisions from imperfect options. The more you handle predicaments, the more you know that if you make a decision that doesn't pan out well you can still survive. In fact, you will learn from it and you will do better the next time with a mindset that is open to discovery. In the *Fast Company* article, "7 Tricks for making good decisions in times of crisis,"[51] Lorten Pratt, Cofounder and Chief Scientist at Quantellia, a firm that makes decision intelligence software, suggests you start with the desired outcome and work your way backward. See yourself getting that outcome and then step by backward step what you need to do to achieve it. When your ego is strong enough to be guided by your core values and mission, yet not so overzealous that you can't acknowledge fault, you will be able to keep your eyes on the outcome you want and increase your chances of getting that outcome.

PART II

9 LEADERSHIP
INTENTIONING TOOLS

·················

CHAPTER 7

AN INTRODUCTION TO THE 9 LEADERSHIP INTENTIONING TOOLS AND HOW TO USE THEM

The Power to Do What?

When I realized that I would have to scale in order to push through to parity, my program morphed into the nonprofit Take The Lead with the resolute mission of preparing and propelling women to take their fair and equal share of leadership positions across all sectors by 2025.[52] I then built a comprehensive program, rooted in research, to back it up. While the initial focus was on helping women embrace their power, I have now realized that the next laser focus must be on what we use that power for, or in other words, our intention.

···

My focus is on intentioning parity—because it won't just happen on its own.

···

This is a program that includes training, coaching, role models, and thought leadership and is more introspective than most traditional leadership programs. It always begins by asking women to stand across an imaginary continuum according to how comfortable they are with power, on a scale from one to ten. We watch as most of them huddle somewhere in the middle. Even women who have come to a training explicitly to hone their leadership skills shrink from acknowledging their power. (Since I began doing this ten years ago, I am happy to say that few now position themselves on the very low end.)

As alarming as it is to me personally, it's understandable: Women are ambivalent about embracing power because we've been conditioned, from television to religion to the workplace, to understand power as an exercise *over* others. The narrative of history has been written in bloody force through wars and the assumption of scarce resources. Men have been the protagonists. And women have been the bit players—the supporting actors, and often the victims of brutality in the archives and books from which we all learn.

But the truth is, *power itself has no attributes.* It is pure energy. I have likened it to a hammer before. Let me expand on the explanation now: You can use it to demolish, destroy, or punish ... or you can use it with equal force to build communities and construct ladders that will help others climb up with you.

In *No Excuses*, I encouraged women to embrace the power they already have and use it intentionally for good: their own good, the good of their families and organizations, the good of the world—and for good as in "forever." I asked them to change how they were thinking about power, to visualize it as the *power to* instead of *power over.*

With that mental shift, I would see the finely crafted masks fall off women's faces, for they no longer need to shield themselves from power. They could uncover and reveal their true selves. They could embrace power with a whole heart in healthy ways. They could choose power over fear. I provided 9 actionable Leadership Power Tools to help women lead effectively.[53] The participants were told they must be willing to state what they will do with their *power to*. In other words, they were encouraged to declare *their intention*. By the end of the program, the women's "power number" on the continuum where they stood earlier trended toward an eight, and in some cases as high as a ten. In every class at least one woman says, not altogether joking, that she's an 11 or a 12. Wow, what progress!

So as we stand here, having been tested by an enormous global challenge, having faced it in our own individual and collective ways, and having seen the extent and potential of our own power, the question from this day forward becomes, *What is your intention? Or better yet, what is your **biggest, boldest** intention?*

This is how the next big shift and my new set of leadership tools focused on intentioning evolved. *Intentioning* is unquestionably a leadership book. One that will turn out an entire corps of female leaders. Never before has a moment been so monumental. So ripe for such an audacious call to action. The confluence of the #metoo movement with the ever-stronger business case for women of all intersectionalities to be lifted into leadership positions ignited a strategic inflection moment that is forcing organizations to rethink leadership and finally provide fair access to it

· ·

Purpose—knowing your "power to what"—is the backbone of intentioning.

· ·

Your purpose is the answer to the question: Your power to do what? It's your moral center and your driver during tough times. Copywriting Addict Alice Hoekstra professes in her piece for Thrive Global that purpose is vital, according to science: "In a new study led by University College London, Princeton University, and Stony Brook University, researchers found that individuals with a sense of purpose live two years longer on average than individuals without a sense of purpose."[54]

What could you do with two years' worth of time? Two years' worth of intentioning? On the heels of spending nearly that much time doing everything in our personal power to survive a deadly virus, we must have some ideas. Let's make our time count. In two years, I will be much closer to seeing my mission of gender parity in leadership manifest. All the while, I will be leading the charge like a woman, which brings us to the start of our Leadership Intentioning Tools playbook.

We've attained a certain height on the rock wall, but there's plenty left to scale. Simultaneously, we've shattered glass ceilings only to see some women fall from the rafters when they were recruited for leadership roles in troubled organizations and weren't any more successful than their male peers were in cleaning up the messes. Unquestionably, my audacious intention of gender parity will require plenty of hard work and smart strategy to be achieved by 2025!

This moment began pre-pandemic and pre-protests over racial injustice and has only been made more urgent because of them. The notion that the future is female has taken hold, not just in t-shirts boldly worn by flaming feminists such as me or in women's magazines that are supposed to assert this, but by pundits and influencers.

Even cheesemaking is decidedly female now![55] Women have been steadily building an "artisan economy" perfecting small-scale production as craft brewers, coffee roasters, knitters, and, yes, cheesemakers. By bringing back these long-lost arts, women are connecting consumers with the products they buy and with the people who make them.

Simultaneously, as both men and women see more gender equality in leadership and women in leadership positions become normalized, attitudes toward women change. According to a December 2017 Harris Poll, half (50 percent) of 2,066 adults aged 18+ said they would "prefer to work at a female-led company over a male-led company." (Of the respondents who preferred a female-led company, 55 percent were women and 46 percent were men.) And 81 percent of women as well as 59 percent of men said,

"When they see women in leadership positions, they're encouraged to believe that they can also have a leadership position."[56]

We're almost halfway to leadership parity, and that, in turn, means that doubling, rather than accepting small incremental increases, is within reach.

As a movement builder, however, I know that we must take the moment "at the flood," as Shakespeare (or maybe his sister) wrote. Because moments don't last, and movements don't move unless people make them do so. The actions required are backed by intention, and the challenge of today is to turn the concept of intention into the action it requires.

••

Intend to and you will—that's *intentioning*. intentioning [in-ten-sh*uh*-ning]

••

There, it's an official dictionary term!

My call to action in *No Excuses* was for women to redefine and embrace their power, and I gave them the tools to do just that. The call to action in *Intentioning* is for women to take the next step. To embrace even higher levels of intention. To *lead like a woman*. And to achieve gender parity by 2025.

My clarion call to women is to refrain from "keeping calm and carrying on" as we've done for so long, and instead to "be bold and *carry out*." There is simply no more time or leeway for apathy, inertia, hesitation, excuses, or giving in to stereotype threats that penalize women who appear powerful for this unequal state of affairs to last another precious moment.

Be Bold and Carry Out—with Intention

My work with women and men during my career has given me extraordinary insight into the nitty-gritty truth of how change is effected for the individual woman, and what systems remain to be changed by using the power of intentioning. Each woman confronts different challenges around age- and race-based discrimination, motherhood, internal doubt, and external judgment that make her journey of embracing her power fraught. But I've learned that there's a secret sauce, a sweet spot, a magic word—whatever you want to call it—that makes all the difference between stasis and success.

Intentioning made the difference for an entrepreneur who, despite being the younger, less experienced partner, was able to realize the value she brought to her company and was subsequently able to negotiate 51 percent ownership.

Intentioning made the difference for the finance program director who made a plan to become a vice president and did so within one year of implementing her plan.

Intentioning made the difference for the nonprofit emerging leader, and the journalist, and the film producer, each of whom set different goals much higher and bolder than they had ever imagined before they joined Take The Lead, thus shifting their power paradigm, and acquiring the skills necessary to thrive in the world while changing it.

What follows in the next chapter are 9 Leadership Intentioning Tools. They can be put into practice immediately. They stand alone and you can also use them in tandem with the original 9 Leadership Power Tools from *No Excuses*. With these tools, you will be even more fully prepared to accomplish not only your own highest and boldest intentions, but you'll be helping all women attain the bold intention of gender parity in leadership across all sectors by 2025.

The VCA Method of Intentioning: Vision, Courage, Action
At its core, effective intentioning consists of three parts.
1. The vision to see clearly what you want to achieve.
2. The courage to go after it.
3. The will to take the actions required to get there. When you're able to set an intention and execute it, you're able to walk, finally, through those parted doors and into your highest and best future.

I have likened the power of intention to the lesson I learned when I was standing, unable to move, on a rickety, swaying wooden suspension bridge across a raging river on the Milford Track in New Zealand. I am terrified of suspension bridges under the best of circumstances. And I had just become aware that I would have to cross 22 of them on the three-day hike I had embarked upon.

My husband trotted across and turned around to laugh at me, adding to my humiliation, as other hikers were lining up behind me waiting for me to cross so they could go next. After a few panicked moments, I realized that I had to do three things: I had to have the vision to fix my eyes clearly on the other side— my intention. I had to muster the courage to believe I could get across. And I had to start putting one foot in front of the other, in front of the other, in front of the other—taking action until I reached my intention.

Vision, courage, and action—those are the parts of the VCA method of intentioning. Sometimes action comes before courage, as it did in part for me. I never lost my fear of suspension bridges, but with each of the 22 I crossed, I gained more courage to know I could do it. Yet in all instances the vision had to come first, or I would have missed the mark. And so it is with the challenges we face while aiming to go about intentioning to create the life and career of our dreams or to achieve anything else we set our minds to.

But there is one more thing you need to know before you can be successful at intentioning. It's another important distinction that too many leadership programs miss and I want you to have full awareness of.

The Difference Between Ambition and Intention

The key difference for you to note is that ambition is the fuel that drives you, while intention takes the fuel and turns it into the action that gets you *there*. Ambition is a state of "I hope, I wish, I want." Intention is a solid belief and action plan of "Heck yes, I will…I see it happening…In fact, I am doing it…There was never a question…I am capable and determined…I have a clear vision of where I want to end up …I have the courage to believe I can do it …And I am taking the action needed to achieve it."

I shared in the introduction to this book that it's always the pebbles that trip you up on the path to leadership, not the mountains. Intentioning allows you to stay focused and elevate your thoughts and, therefore, your goals, whether it's a pebble you encounter or a mountain. Even when you stumble, as all of us will from time to time, your vision will remain clearly focused on the intention. Sustain the courage to believe you can do it and keep putting one foot in front of the other, taking action till you reach your goal.

··

To master intentioning, you need a willing mindset and a user's manual. That's exactly what this book provides in its combination of introductory chapters, its 9 Leadership Intentioning Tools, and the resources listed to help you on your way.

··

If you are ready to practice intentioning to elevate your career success and to lead the life you desire, the following pages will show you how:

- Intentioning prepares you to lead change, be change, and sustain change.
- Intentioning helps you to remain aware of the consequences of your actions and to flex as needed.
- Intentioning 100 percent improves your impact in meetings and presentations.
- Intentioning is a proactive practice that builds habits to sustain your leadership journey and helps you avoid derailers or "power demons" as I non-affectionately call them.
- Intentioning allows you to turn your obstacles into assets.

Finally, through the potent stories of "Intentional Women," we'll elaborate on each of the 9 Leadership Intentioning Tools, adding tips for implementing them and practice exercises for each.

Are you excited to apply your power *to* energies to your intention? I know I'm excited to see you do it. Why? A glut of self-help books targeting women in the past decade have been stuck on the tired question of *whether* we can have it all, either pushing us to make a grab for a laundry list of goals ("Motherhood!" "Corner office!" "Thriving sex life!") or accept limitations. Aren't you done with having your very existence defined and determined by the old, musty, leather coat of suppressive language aimed at dragging you down?

Intentioning steps outside of that old paradigm that's become a prison. Intentioning will show how to change the institutions in which we work and live so that women and men together can lead healthier, happier, and more productive lives. It's a fresh, liberating approach to reaching gender parity in leadership and to living life in general.

Intentioning will help you dream impossible dreams, then give you the actionable tools to achieve them.

Come along with me. My impossible dream? Women will Take The Lead to reach parity by 2025, for their own good, for everyone's good as in the good of the world, and yes, for good as in "forever."

I intend it.

I see it.

It will happen.

Let's go for it.

THE 9 LEADERSHIP INTENTIONING TOOLS

••••••••••••••

The Self Definitional Leadership Intentioning Tools

1. **Uncover Yourself** ... because what sets you apart is what gets you ahead, and the keys to your best future are already in your hands.
2. **Dream Up** ... because if your dreams don't scare you, they're not big enough.
3. **Believe in the Infinite Pie** ... because when we use our power to build rather than rule over others, we learn that the more there is, the more there is.

The Counterintuitive Leadership Intentioning Tools

4. **Modulate Confidence** ... because self-doubt can have a positive value.
5. **Strike Your Own Damn Balance (and Love Your Stress)** ... because ultimately you get to choose what matters to you and unchoose the rest. Pay no attention to the man behind the curtain telling you you're supposed to be unhappy.
6. **Build Social Capital** ... because relationships are everything and will ultimately help you as much as educational qualifications or work experience.

The Systems Change Leadership Intentioning Tools

7. **Be Unreasonable** ... because sometimes you have to break the rules and invent new ones to get where you want to go.
8. **Unpack Implicit Bias and Turn Its Effects on Its Head** ... because you can make its effects your superpowers.
9. **Clang Your Symbols** ... because symbols create meaning, and when you create meaning, you bring others into the story, and that's the most essential function of leadership.

CHAPTER 8

·················

THE 9 LEADERSHIP INTENTIONING TOOLS

These tools are designed to guide you as you Lead Like a Woman, radically redefining power at a deep and authentic level, so that you can embrace your power to elevate your highest intentions and stay on the path to achieve them with discipline and focus.

You know that the three elements of intention are vision, courage, and action (VCA). You know that your ambition is the fuel, but your intention is what utilizes the fuel and drives your actions to completion—the actualization of your intention.

Because your intentions are rooted in your essential core values and purpose, working toward them will fill you with energy and the joy of knowing that you are standing in your integrity, with the skills and tools to manifest those intentions. I love Frederick Buechner's characterization that this is "the place where your deep gladness and the world's deep hunger meet."

You are ready. You have all that you need to take you where you want to go. And I am here to keep cheering you on.

These tools are more about mindset than skills, but you will acquire and develop skills as you practice them. As stated earlier, they can be used alone or along with the 9 Leadership Power Tools from *No Excuses*. These new tools are grouped into the same three categories as the original 9 Leadership Power Tools. The groupings include *self-definitional tools, counterintuitive tools*, and *systems change tools.*

Each of these Leadership Intentioning Tools helps you gain new insights to question conventional wisdom and culturally learned behaviors that have held us back and that we often use by default to make the most important decisions in our lives. By reading specific examples of women who have used these tools to boost intentioning in their own lives, we break down assumptions that do not serve us and build up our power to lead and to live our highest and best lives while advancing parity for all women.

Because I want you to have the benefit of this wisdom at your fingertips whenever you need it, I've created a downloadable sheet for The 9 Leadership Intentioning Tools that you can find at www.intentioningbook.com. You will see a mini wallet-sized version at this link too. Many people post the longer form by their computers and carry the mini one with them in their pocket or purse. Refer to it as needed. It will serve as your personal coach and guide.

In fact, it would be helpful to review the summary now before we explore each Leadership Intentioning Tool individually. These brief descriptions on page 86 show at a glance how each tool connects to the others to form a coherent strategy for your success.

So are you ready? Here goes!

THE SELF-DEFINITIONAL
LEADERSHIP INTENTIONING TOOLS

Leadership Intentioning Tool #1: Uncover Yourself . . . because what sets you apart is what gets you ahead, and the keys to your best future are already in your hands.

> *"One of the criticisms I've faced over the years is that I'm not aggressive enough or assertive enough or maybe somehow, because I'm empathetic, it means I'm weak. I totally rebel against that. I refuse to believe that you cannot be both compassionate and strong."*
> —JACINDA ARDERN, PRIME MINISTER OF NEW ZEALAND[57]

Ardern has become a role model for so many people. Her exemplary handling of COVID-19 led her to the global stage as an example of the kind of leadership needed in such a crisis. She exemplifies the framework of leading like a woman described in chapter 5.

But given the pressures of culturally learned behaviors that women have been praised or punished for, shifting to the "lead like a woman" paradigm can be hard. It is necessary for many of us to peel back those layers we've piled on over time either to cloak or differently define ourselves, and actually reveal our true selves. That can be painful. It can feel risky, terrifying even. Because when we change our behavior, we may fear losing the love of those who are important to us.

Yet the plain fact is that the best leaders know themselves deeply, as Ardern apparently does. Their values and actions reflect authentically who they are, not someone else's idea of who they should be. And they know who they are because they have uncovered themselves for themselves. They are comfortable in their own skins. Their authenticity builds trust, and trust is at the heart of effective leadership.

••

Uncovering yourself can take time to accomplish fully, so be gentle with yourself.

••

As Brené Brown says, "You either walk inside your story and own it or you stand outside your story and hustle for your worthiness."

It is worth the effort. For me, it was liberating. It was as if I were breathing fully for the first time. I felt I was living in integrity with myself, and I discovered such a feeling makes the rest of life's decisions flow easily.

In my mid-30s, my teenage marriage, like most teenage marriages, was coming apart. But I was terrified that if I made a move, I would lose my family, my friends, and my kids who were and are the center of my life. I felt powerless. Stuck.

I had tried so hard to convince myself that the life I had chosen at 16 was what I wanted because I had been acculturated to think it was what I wanted. I longed to fit in, not to feel "different" or "other." But in truth, it had never been a comfortable fit, hard as I tried to make it so. It was a charade.

I was awakening to the reality that I had never ever, not once, chosen my life's path from my own intention. The choices I had made weren't choices at all but rather the results of ceding my power to forces outside myself. That was a shocker.

I had been covering. You might know that term for trying to fit in even when you don't. It's a pretty good description of what many women experience, working in institutions designed by men for men 200 years ago. I honestly think this is one reason why you see such an upsurge in female entrepreneurs and why I observed previously that the real competition companies have in retaining female talent is not from other companies but from women themselves choosing to start their own businesses or to drop out of the workforce entirely if they are financially able to do so.

I had to come to terms with myself. I had to *un*cover the true me and acknowledge that it was time to take a different turn in my life. I had to own it, however uncomfortable it was to shed the leathered outer layer I had constructed based on other people's ideas about me. I had to show up as my authentic self. What a relief when I finally did!

Equally important, I had to realize that no one else could do it for me. That what I needed was accessible if I had the vision to see it and the courage to take the actions required to get it.

••••••••••••••••••••••••••••

I had to become an intentional woman.

••••••••••••••••••••••••••••

I'm still working on that every day. I slip back into old habits from time to time because, frankly, it can be easier than owning responsibility for myself.

If what it means to uncover yourself is to peel away the layers of experiences and beliefs that do not come from your authentic self, then how many layers must you shed to get to your raw being—you in all your originality, expression, core values, emotion, vision, evolution, potential and contributions, beauty, and legacy?

"Covering" in the workplace refers to the many layers we put on ourselves to fit in, to get ahead, or to be seen as more mainstream. New York University law professor Kenji Shoshino, who is Asian-American, identified this phenomenon as detrimental to workforce efforts to promote inclusion. He notes that people may cover by adapting their appearance, refraining from advocating, standing up, or speaking out for others, affiliating or not with a particular identity group, or associating with people based on their proximity to the norms accepted in their particular setting.[58] We know women who won't display pictures of their children in their office in order to avoid being penalized for being a mom. This is a clear and relatable example of covering for many of us.

Other people refer to covering as the "masks we wear from an early age." These metaphorical masks (not to be confused with the actual masks required for protection in the era of COVID) derive from limiting beliefs that our parents or other family units instilled in us. In fact, studies have found that 81 percent of employees say that they cover their identities, or some aspects of them, all or some of the time. This is true of 66 percent of women, 83 percent of LGBTQ individuals, 79 percent of Blacks, and even 45 percent of straight white men.[59] Yet we all do a better job and are happier when we can fully be ourselves and not feel as if we have to hide something.

Have you been covering yourself? How and why? What would it feel like to uncover yourself? What are the risks and rewards? What would you hope to achieve with your authentic power and intention? What would you fully, joyfully manifest?

9 Power Demons

Recognizing obstacles to your intentioning practice is part of uncovering. The very nature of a "demon"—and yes, I'm intentionally attaching a diabolical face to these obstacles—is to torment. If you are tormented, you certainly cannot devote your energies to intentioning a life of purpose and fulfillment. I encourage you to pause and contemplate the power demons that may be preventing you from releasing the covers that have shielded you thus far from courageously seeing and revealing your true self.

By the way, when you have completed this book, you will be aware of 81 power demons. Here are some that are especially dangerous to your desire to uncover yourself.

- Not identifying your core values
- Not having a vision
- Lacking focus
- Languishing in a state of fear rather than stepping into courage
- Straying from qualities such as competence, creativity, intuition, vulnerability, vision, self-awareness, connection, and authenticity in order to adopt more masculine qualities
- Skipping steps related to your own well-being
- Putting off the thought of leaving a legacy
- Dismissing being authentic for playing it safe
- Measuring words, *not* intentioning

INTENTIONAL WOMAN

How Debra Sterling, Founder and CEO of GoldieBlox, Uncovered Herself and Created a New Way to Encourage Girls to Build Things

Debra Sterling started GoldieBlox because she wanted to interest girls in engineering, but deep down what propelled her was women's equality. As she will tell you, that is her singular passion.

GoldieBlox is an award-winning children's multimedia company disrupting the pink aisle in toy stores globally and challenging gender stereotypes with the world's first girl engineer character.[60] In the same way Disney has created "princesses," Debra wants girls to live out the "maker" fantasy, with help from GoldieBlox building kits, apps, books, and a YouTube series. Her impossible dream is a global multimedia franchise so every girl can look up to the various multicultural Goldies. (Of course, I use the word "impossible" in the Audrey Hepburn sense of it as she once famously said, "Nothing is impossible; the word itself says I'm possible.")

But Debra didn't arrive at the idea for GoldieBlox without uncovering key elements of herself first.

She was born in Los Angeles and had a natural ability for drawing, cartooning, and painting. Her parents dreamed of her becoming an actress, but she was planning to pursue her artistic talents when she was accepted into Stanford University ("almost making my mother faint"). While at school, she decided to try an engineering class.

I chuckled when Debra told me she was the girly princess who accidentally stumbled into engineering and found that she liked it. She calls engineering "problem solving." The only aspect of engineering Debra didn't like was that there were so few women.

Once, in a perspectival drawing class, she was having trouble with an assignment. A cocky male teaching assistant looked at her work and asked the class to raise their hands if they thought she should "pass" the course. Humiliated, she walked out and cried, resolving to quit engineering as a major. A classmate named Micah—a man who stepped up to support her—talked her out of the idea, encouraging her to continue.

Later, while talking with a female friend who observed that little girls didn't get building toys to play with and learn from, Debra had a lightbulb moment. She knew exactly what she could do to rectify the lack of women in the profession.

"We women doubt ourselves so much," Debra explains. "From lack of role models to messages from the media, we're often quick to think we are not able to do something. What enabled me to get past my self-doubt is that I had the breakthrough idea that if girls from a young age were socialized with engineering toys and tools, it would change their world."

In other words, she had identified her intention. And soon she was off intentioning GoldieBlox into being. "My focus is bigger than myself. That supersedes any barrier. Join in the mission or get out of the way!" she said with conviction.

Debra has grown into leading like a woman after being a self-prescribed "hustler running a million miles an hour." By her own admission, she mimicked the male dominated start-up behavior she thought was necessary as cover while she was a budding entrepreneur. It was perfectly understandable of course; Debra had only male engineering role models up to that point. But she started working with an executive coach and discovered new ways to lead more effectively. She learned how to be comfortable with herself as a female leader. She ultimately became more transparent, a better communicator, and a leader who makes smart but quick decisions.

Debra's industry, like so many others, faced challenges during the pandemic. The supply chain was upended with the closure of retail outlets that carried her products. Pregnant with her second child and planning for his birth, she began quickly to onboard a new executive leadership team to ensure the company would achieve its goals while she was on maternity leave. Her pregnancy became a forcing function prompting her to prioritize key hires. This strategy paid off because Debra had the experienced team she needed in place and was ready to pivot business operations when it came time to weather the storm. They put a stronger focus on creating educational content for families with kids who were out of school. They launched a virtual summer camp in partnership with the American Association for the Advancement of Science and Lyda Hill Philanthropies, and they produced content with female STEM professionals safely from their homes to inspire girls to get into STEM.

Debra adds, "This is a moment of reckoning for all women. Finally, gender equality is becoming more of a priority for businesses, venture capital, and philanthropy. I am hopeful that we will see more investment dollars directed toward advancing women. My advice is to take advantage. In the past, I've shied away from opportunities 'for women' because I thought to myself, *I don't want to be handed something just because I'm a woman. I want to win opportunities regardless of my gender.* I no longer think that way. The truth is, women are afforded so many fewer opportunities than men, that the time has come where we can and should claim them, regardless of how they are framed. And we should not second guess ourselves or feel inferior in any way for capitalizing on this moment in time. It's long overdue."

You can call Debra's an "Uncover Yourself success story." I intend that you will have such a success story someday soon too.

Leadership Intentioning Tool #2: Dream Up . . .

because if your dreams don't scare you, they're not big enough.

*The future belongs to those who believe in the beauty
of their dreams.*—ELEANOR ROOSEVELT

I'll say it again in case you missed it the first few times: If your dreams don't scare you, they're not big enough. Level up. Scale up. Woman up. If you can dream it, you can do it. All things are possible with intentioning. I say "dream up" because too often we limit ourselves.

I realize that the dream up mindset can only take you so far if you aren't seeing results. You may burn out and beg off from your dream when you get distracted, disrupted, or disturbed. After all, you're only human. But when such obstacles present themselves, it is often helpful to think of your intention as an impossible dream. Then it becomes even sweeter when your dream comes true, which it often does if you use the three powers of intention: when you have a clear *vision*, you have *courage* to believe you can do it, and you are taking *action* every day to make it happen.

For some of us, intention takes a while to manifest since there are many choices to consider. For others of us, visualizing our impossible dream happens early. Shellye Archambeau, for example, told me over dinner when we met at a Diversity Woman conference that she knew when she was a teen and first learned that there was such a thing as a CEO that it was her intention to become one. And step by intentional step, as she shares in her book *Unapologetically Ambitious: Take Risks, Break Barriers, and Create Success on Your Own Terms*, she became the CEO of MetricStream, a technology company. This is rare for a woman and rarer still for a Black woman. Now she sits on the boards of Fortune 500 companies. Her book is a great read about how she did it.[61]

I told you that my impossible dream is gender parity in leadership for all women by 2025. Many people have said that is impossible (and have meant the term differently than I do, as in "they think it will never happen"). But I tell them that my work for women's equality and parity started decades ago. If I could live the 70 to 150 years longer that they say it will take, I would be happy to do so. But the odds aren't good, so we have to get it done while I'm still alive to see it.

Okay? Are you with me? Good. Because that "dream up" mindset is key.

Dreaming up is the demonstrable intersection between ambition and intention. Remember that ambition is *I hope, I wish, I want*. Intention is *I will, I am, I already see it happening*.

Still, it's also true that ambitious women are often disparaged while ambitious men are lauded. So intentional women will likely have to contend with many roadblocks and naysayers.

Casting aspersions on women's ambition is in fact an intentional, though often unconscious, cultural pressure for women to stay in their humble place. That place downplays women's ambition so much so that it often can't graduate to intention.

Journalist Christina Tapper, a participant in Take The Lead's 50 Women Can Change the World in Journalism,[62] shared a conversation she had with an executive who asked her what she wanted to do next in her career. "I want to remain in leadership to develop and shape strategy, cultivate talent and big ideas, experiment more to stretch the imagination within storytelling, and do it in a more inclusive and nurturing environment," she said. "Well," the executive responded and not in a positive way, "that's very ambitious of you." Christina's comeback was epic. "Though his tone was trash, the exec figured out exactly who I am. 'Yes, sir. I am *very ambitious*, I said. 'Thanks for the confirmation. I'll own that.'"[63]

That sound you hear is me clapping loudly. Because I think that Christina was actually describing intention.

Remember, ambition is the fuel. Intention uses the fuel to drive to the goal.

Here's when it clicked for me that intention is necessary to activate ambition. I noticed that the approximately 20 percent gender pay gap matches the approximately 20 percent differential in women's valuation of their own worth as discovered both in research and real life. The job markets website ZipRecruiter crunched the numbers to compare the salaries women ask for versus the salaries men with the same qualifications ask for when applying for the same jobs. They found women ask for, on average, $11,103 less than men.[64]

Similarly, when the Women's Campaign Fund asked women candidates why they decided to take the plunge and run for public office, the typical answer was, "Someone asked."[65] I concluded that what holds women back is not the lack of ambition but an intention gap. While little boys seem to jump out of the womb knowing they own the world, women often don't perceive themselves as having intentioning agency as a birthright. But we can all uncover that sense of agency and worthiness once we realize our intentions are actually there waiting to be released.

This behavior is not biologically determined but it is gendered through cultural learning. The way women are socialized around intention is the missing piece in solving the seemingly intractable puzzle of these disparities. Implicit bias and well-trodden structural barriers lower our intentions, especially the vision of what we can do or be, and equally important, what we *want* to do or be. That's a phenomenon we will discuss more fully in Leadership Intentioning Tool #8, where I'll show you how to turn those bias-caused mental adaptations into your superpowers.

. . . .

Understanding intention can help us rewire our instinct to limit it. Practicing intention carries a power all its own that you can put to use daily.

. . . .

Charlotte Jorst, an entrepreneur who now identifies herself as an athlete to denote her focus on her current passion of award-winning horsewomanship, is also the serial entrepreneur founder of the popular Skagen Denmark watch company[66] and after selling it, the Kastel Denmark sun protection active clothing line. She talked with me about starting her businesses. More recently, though, she has been through a divorce she didn't see coming and dealing with the challenges of integrating that reality into her life while staying true to her own purpose and intentions. She says:

"Setting goals is tough. Especially if they are high goals, you don't know if you'll ever reach them. You have to enjoy the journey, *everything* about the journey. The places it takes you, the people you meet, the kindness, the friendships, the hardships. Sometimes learning to love the hardships is key. If you want to get in better shape you'll have to learn to love being out of breath. So when you're out of breath you'll have to tell yourself, 'I love to be out of breath.' Changing how you think about the obstacles will make you continue through them and if you love the journey the ultimate goal becomes less important; you are already living your life the way you want."

EXERCISE

Here are three surefire ways to allow your ambition to fuel your intention to Dream UP big time, while enjoying the journey. Because if you don't enjoy it, it's probably not meant to be your true intention:

- Research your worth and document it. Do the deep inventory on your talents, your experiences, and your capacities. Discover your worth in the marketplace through websites like ZipRecruiter, 81 Cents, and PayScale. Don't second-guess the evidence and don't hold back because you feel there are things you don't yet know. Look at what you had to do to get where you are. How well you adapted to or created something new is as important as your formal learning. You must value yourself to have clarity of your intentions in alignment with your values.

- Allow yourself to dream those impossible dreams. Be bold about your vision for the future and push the parameters wide. Is your next step to run for office, start a business, aim for the executive suite, solve global warming? Whatever it is, you can't increment your way to success. Setting big intentions and accomplishing 80 percent is vastly more fruitful than setting smaller goals you can easily accomplish and reaching 100 percent.

> • Above all, listen to your own clarion call to action and ignore the naysayers. Wake up every morning and write down at least one step you will take that day toward achieving your bold intention. Look back on it in the evening and give yourself credit for what you have done. Don't let what you haven't done deter you; instead learn from it. Remember there is always a way. Maybe you just haven't found it yet.

9 Power Demons
- Feeding into distractions
- Looking for detours
- Negative thinking
- Undermining someone else's dream
- Thinking dreams are for others with more time, opportunity, money, and access
- Trading in happiness for what feels normal
- Not owning your decisions
- Dwelling in self-pity
- Dwelling in the past

INTENTIONAL WOMAN

Pianist and Composer Marina Arsenijevic

Marina Arsenijevic is in many respects my archetype of the intentional woman. She is an international award-winning pianist and composer and star of the Emmy-nominated public television program *Marina at West Point: Unity through Diversity*.

But it was quite a long road spanning thousands of miles, literally and metaphorically, from her initial vision to achieving her intention, with plenty of courageous actions in between. I first met Marina when she reached out to me after she had joined some women in the building where I live in New York to watch the livestream of Take

The Lead's launch event we held at Arizona State University's Grady Gammage Auditorium in Tempe, Arizona, on February 19, 2014.

Marina Arsenijevic is one of those rare individuals who from an early age knew exactly what she wanted to do in life and did it. Dreaming up came naturally. She has employed several tools of intentioning, but it's almost like "dream up" is her brand and she's the compelling ambassador for the concept.

Marina had a disciplined upbringing—and discipline would stand her in solid intentioning stead. Though her father played guitar and her mother was a talented singer, they didn't encourage their only child to pursue her musical passion. They thought it was not a practical career path in war-torn Serbia where she was born and raised. Her father was a professional soccer player who decided he needed to have a more secure life and became the head of the local water company. Her mother was a lawyer in charge of pension funds in communist Yugoslavia.

Marina fell in love with the piano at age four when she heard an accompanist play in her ballet class. She was relentless in her desire to pursue this passion, but her family would not comply. While her father was building pipelines for a company in Italy, however, he brought Marina some miniature plastic pianos. She then collected over 100 of the small plastic replicas until she finally convinced her parents to buy her a real one.

She was nine when her father purchased a standup piano, which took up a lot of room in their small apartment. She began practicing and practicing, day after day. She attended music school in the evening, and returned home at eight o'clock every night, in time to do her homework for her regular classes, go to bed, and get up early the next morning to start all over again. She was a prodigy but more importantly, her internal drive to learn and perform could not be stopped. Her first audience consisted of 800 students from her day school—that taste of performing live is a memory she has carried her whole life.

She loved the stage and the communication she felt with the audience. She was euphoric as she took a bow. Looking into her classmates' eyes, she saw two reactions that would shape her life. The first was happiness and gratitude for her performance. For children in a country on the brink of war, it was something positive that many of them had never experienced. But she also saw something else that frightened and saddened her: envy. She knew at that moment that her pursuit would be a solitary and sometimes lonely road in which she would be sacrificing friendships for her craft.

Marina's Russian professor, a famous pianist, informed her parents of her rare gift. "She is extremely talented," he said. "We can send her to a conservatory in Moscow." Her parents did not agree. They wanted her to experience life, not be isolated day and night practicing away from the rest of the world. They were supportive but like most parents, they wanted their child to have a stable, normal existence. They thought she wouldn't be able to support herself with her music as Marina was a free spirit. Her parents wanted her to think about starting her own family instead.

Then Marina won a piano competition in Rome, Italy, when she was 17 years old. The prize money was more than three months of her parents' salary. "You see," she said to them. "You were opposing my choices and here I am bringing you all this money."

No one, not parents, teachers, or community members, could dissuade her from becoming a musician; in fact, their opposition was fodder for her resolute intentioning. She was determined to prove them all wrong.

Marina's father knew how hard it was to pursue this dream because of his own unrealized dream of becoming a famous soccer player. He also knew that women in his country had a particularly hard time making it in conventional jobs and were prone to attacks by the media and the community if they did anything outside of the norm. To be outspoken in Serbia was dangerous; to be outspoken as a woman in Serbia could be suicidal.

But Marina was not one to play by conventional rules. She knew music was a male-dominated world in Eastern Europe, and so she developed a powerful piano technique in which she elevates her body off the piano bench while playing. This gives her the advantage of transferring strength to her arms, and along with her legendary finger strength, puts her on equal ground with her larger-handed male competitors. This technique contributed to her becoming the reigning champion for years in Yugoslavian music competitions and winning six international piano competitions in Italy and Macedonia. She went on to perform with every major orchestra in Eastern and Central Europe.

For many years, Marina felt her gift to the world was the moving music she played for audiences, but this would become only the tip of the iceberg. Playing other composers' music was one vehicle for her message of unity, but it was the music she would compose herself that would calm a nation that had been at war for so many years.

Writing original music led Marina to an even higher intention: using her music as a unifying force that permeates all religions and ideologies. She knew no matter where a person is from, music is something that speaks of their trials, obstacles, joys, and sorrows. There is a power in music that can for a moment, bring people together during a performance. It is a way of understanding and communicating without malice, hatred, or killing.

She wanted her music to unite the Yugoslav people and remind them that they all had a common heritage. Marina took a risk and during the height of the civil wars she performed Muslim and Christian music with the Serbian Radio and Television Symphony Orchestra at Kosovo's largest hall, the 11,000-seat Boro Ramiz Center in Prishtina, to a standing-room-only crowd of both Muslims and Christians. Even though war was raging on the outside, there was not a single violent incident inside during her concert. She had unified people, even if for one night.

Television production companies offered Marina blank contracts, the kind reserved only for major athletes and artists. She refused because these companies were controlled by extremist political figures who wanted nothing but to use her as a pawn. They were shocked when this 21-year-old declined their money.

She knew her mission was creating unity through her music in a diverse and divided climate, and that by aligning herself politically, that dream could potentially be destroyed. The extremists had her barred from performing on television, but this only ignited a brighter fire, because she knew in her heart that the people wanted to hear more from her and that her music was uplifting and affecting a nation in a way that war never could.

When bombs began falling in Belgrade, Marina was called to the national television station to help calm the people. The masses loved and trusted her. She performed another seventy-five standing-room-only concerts anywhere she could—shopping centers, hotels, and music halls. She continued to blend ethnic music and cultural rhythms with Muslim and Christian melodies seamlessly into her performances. The popular *TV Magazine* wrote: "God gave her the look of a model, the talent of an exquisite artist, and the flawless political skill of a chess master. She has an ability to communicate with diverse peoples and nations, which even great diplomats would envy."

Finally, in June 1999, she decided to premiere her composition, "Kosovo," at the National Museum in Belgrade. It was the pinnacle of her work weaving Christian and Muslim melodies into one composition. There was not a dry eye in the house as the people wept for their lost united, multicultural Yugoslavia.

Marina had to leave the country the next day for her own safety. She made her way to the US embassy in Budapest and thereafter to the United States, where she was allowed to stay on an artist visa. She was not looking for asylum or to become a U.S. citizen initially. She loved her country, and she knew she needed to continue her journey of providing music as a unifying force that had brought understanding and peace to her homeland. But America represented hope and provided the freedom to spread her message to an even wider base without judgment or opposition.

Her subsequent decision to stay in the U.S. was not without regret. She had left her family behind. She had traveled with just one suitcase into the unknown, all because she had a mission to complete, one she was unwilling to give up. She began to play at churches and music halls. She performed music people were familiar with to get their attention, but her desire to play her own music and spread her message of unity could not be quelled. Despite many rejections, it was in her heart and soul not to give up. She wanted to change the world with her music, and whenever she performed people were moved and touched. So she knew she was on the right mission.

Marina never covered herself or her dream up intention!

And as often happens when someone knows her intention so deeply, her world took a turn to help actualize it. While playing in a small Steinway showroom in Michigan in 2013, Marina met the program director from the Detroit PBS station along with several other cultural movers and shakers. After they heard her play, they said, "We think you are right for Carnegie Hall."

Five months later, on a brutal New York winter evening, Marina played at the famed institution musicians everywhere have aspired to perform in. She followed that performance with a second Carnegie Hall concert in which she played a mixture of traditional classical and her own new music.

She finally got her biggest break when some of her music was performed with an ensemble of the West Point Band and the West Point Cadet Glee Club on PBS. This "Unity Through Diversity" concert was her dream come true. After it aired, Marina was touted as someone with the beauty of a "James Bond" leading lady and a powerful musical technique that hit audiences like a "Balkan thunderbolt." In 2003, she performed her original arrangement of "America the Beautiful" for Laura Bush and Cherie Blair, along with 2,000 guests at a First Ladies' lunch.

That set the stage for many other opportunities to take her message of unity in diversity to larger platforms. She performed a multicity concert tour in the U.S. and Canada to gain awareness and humanitarian aid for the orphans and children of Eastern Europe. After the fall of Communism in Yugoslavia, Marina returned to her homeland and played in Serbia to over 300,000 fans who flocked to hear the music that had soothed them through troubled times before. Her people never forgot her and what she had provided to them through her moving musical talents.

Marina has a special place in her heart for her famous countryman, Nikola Tesla. She performed her original work, "Tesla's Journey," at the 2013 dedication of her Nikola Tesla statue at Tesla Wardenclyffe Laboratory in Long Island. She continues to compose music that commemorates his life and her "Tesla Rhapsody" debuted in 2015, performed by orchestras both in the U.S. and Europe.

In 2014, Marina received the Ellis Island Medal of Honor. Another of the recipients was an 83-year-old professor and historian. The professor had left her position in New York to go to Yugoslavia in the 1990s to become the Minister of Information. She had seen Marina perform her second concert at Carnegie Hall and wrote her a beautiful letter in which she said, "I can see you can reach very high, big highs in this country, but never forget where you came from. Many people have assimilated, and they lost themselves. If you forget, then no one will value you."

They met again at the dedication of the statue of Nikola Tesla in Long Island. The professor approached Marina and asked, "Do you remember me?" Marina did remember the professor fondly. "Well, you see, you didn't forget where you came from and that's why you have this whole circle," the professor told her.

The professor subsequently gave Marina a book she had written about Mileva Maric, the first wife of Albert Einstein. Marina began reading it and could not put it down. It was unbelievable that Mileva, a woman who helped Einstein so much, was not recognized for her contributions. Only one little plaque on the building where she lived remembers her, stating simply, "This was the home of the first wife of Albert Einstein." In other books written about the life of Albert Einstein, there are usually just two paragraphs about Mileva. Einstein had two children with her, and she was his intellectual partner, instrumental in the development of his theories, including the theory of relativity. Marina was so moved by what she had read, she helped the professor get her book published in the United States.

Marina is an intentional woman who sees herself not so much as a leader but as an inspiration. She drives people to her vision and message of unity and understanding knowing they will embrace it when they experience it. Well, I say she is a highly intentional leader, since in my view a leader is someone who gets stuff done. And Marina certainly does that.

No wonder she was chosen to perform at West Point to honor the seventy-second anniversary of the Liberation of Auschwitz and was awarded Serbia's highest diplomatic honor, the Knighthood of St. Sava for Diplomatic Pacifism.

As I shared in chapter 3, Marina did not allow COVID-19's power demons to prevent her from dreaming up even further. In fact, the pandemic's disruption spurred her to greater creativity and higher intentions. While live performances were cancelled, she prepared a multicultural celebratory program, "Unity Through Diversity," as a Symphony Pops concert series for local orchestras with the United States Army Field Band. She recorded new music nonstop and posted on her burgeoning social media platforms that now have over half a million followers. She also created a full home studio, became her own producer using the best recording and lighting equipment, and found new artists to collaborate with. Her music today is reaching more people than ever.

Marina has a message for women trying to dream up. She believes that you must define what you are about. Many women don't want to dig inside themselves that deeply. They are surrounded by messages in their homes and communities about who they should be, but they must understand who they are first. When you understand who you are in the most authentic way, you must then be disciplined enough to work on yourself or on your craft, every single day. Marina says that discipline is sometimes not creative or fun. She still lives a very disciplined life, and she believes that it has been one of the greatest tools of her success.

Knowing yourself and your passion along with proper discipline and the right mentors and coaches can allow women to take their places at the table, and not be lost in obscurity like Einstein's first wife.

Marina adds: "With all the changes in society and the development of women's equality at all levels, they need to understand that in all situations, they can do it by themselves and not be limited by past norms. Rather than taking a back seat, men and women should ride together sharing the steering wheel and taking the lead when opportunity presents itself. I have been helped by women who were more successful than me at the time. They were an excellent source of understanding, from a female perspective, on what was lacking in my own self-confidence or to gain a fuller realization of my potential. It is valuable to seek role models. You will learn a lot about yourself in the process."

And her West Point concert? As of the end of 2020, it had been telecast 550 times to 170.3 million viewers and is the longest running concert on the PBS network.[67] That's what the drive to Dream Up will get you.

Leadership Intentioning Tool #3: Believe in the Infinite Pie ...

because when we use our power to build *with* rather than rule *over* others, we learn that the more there is, the more there is.

> *"Each time a woman stands up for herself, without knowing it, possibly without claiming it, she stands up for all women."*— Maya Angelou

If I help you and you help me, we both end up with more influence, better ideas, and lots more of whatever we set out to achieve. Going it alone will never create big systemic change. Going it alone isn't strategically wise or necessary. Or as Dr. Nancy O'Reilly, whose story I'll tell you more about later in this chapter, would say—actually did say in her book of this name—we are "In This Together."

Here's why I liken this particular tool to a pie. A chocolate cheesecake, actually. The analogy is a little hokey but humor me.

A few years back, my chocolate marble cheesecake won first prize in a charity chocolate-tasting contest in Arizona. A number of attendees asked whether I shared recipes, implying that I might want to hoard it. I wondered, *Is anyone so needy as to hold onto the miniscule amount of power conferred by a cheesecake recipe?* Needless to say, I smiled and gave the recipe to anyone who asked.

Soon it seemed like half the population of Phoenix was baking that chocolate cheesecake. It occurred to me that another amateur chef could enter the same dessert in the contest next time. But one year later, my chocolate marble cheesecake won first prize again. Apparently, there is no finite cheesecake, um, pie. That principle is one of the bedrocks of the paradigm shift in how we define and claim power on our own terms in order to elevate the intention to lead. Power *over*, as you will recall, assumes that the pie of resources is finite so we must fight over the crumbs. But we must realize that in an economy based on brains not brawn, there is no limit to human intelligence, love, or ingenuity to create more of whatever we need. Our capability for innovation to solve problems is infinite. Think about the medical innovations alone brought about by the pandemic, for example. Aside from the rapid acceptance of previously resisted telemedicine, the COVID vaccines are one obvious innovation. Researchers had been working on genetic sequencing mRNA for years, but the pandemic spurred rapid application to create the vaccines that are conquering COVID. Because of that advance researchers believe they might have the key to curing cancer or treating chronic diseases.[68]

And women are great at baking more pies in any case.

By sharing my life's work, I know I will reach many more people than if I hold it close to my vest, fearing someone would steal the ideas. I suppose I could have made a good business out of my research and the resulting teachings without feeling an obligation to take it further. But I have had the incredible opportunity to see and be part of great social movements. So I know that together, and with the organization Take The Lead, we can enlarge the women's leadership pie faster and better than any one of us could do alone. It's trite to say this is how we change the world, but it's true.

I resonate with Minda Harts' introduction to her popular book *The Memo: What Women of Color Need to Know to Secure a Seat at the Table*[69] in which she talks about the reason for writing it: "My curiosity was larger than my fear, and I didn't want to see another woman of color crawl through her disappointments in the workplace and have no one ever acknowledge them! I was tired of the workplace being separate and far from equal. I was exhausted from the labels and the BS. And, I know we need to make more people aware of how difficult securing our seat at the table can be—I had to write my story and tell the stories of other women of color. And even though most people don't want to admit it, we can't talk about advancing women of color, or the future of work for that matter, and not address race and the history of this country."

The point is that Minda could have taken what she learned about being successful as a Black woman in the workplace and garnered a top leadership position for herself. There would have been nothing wrong with that. But by believing in the infinite pie principle, and intentioning how she could help her sisters, she has fostered the success of a growing number of Black women, and her generosity to others has made her a much-admired thought leader.

I'm a practical activist. I want my work to have impact that is not just meaningful to me, but also, moves the dial toward my life's purpose—my intentioning—of equality and justice for all women: for you, our daughters, and our granddaughters. That's the legacy I want to leave, the passion that propels my work. That's why I cofounded Take The Lead, to have an organization and a movement that can reach many more people and live after me. I draw energy and joy from seeing the results of our collective work to redefine power so women can embrace it authentically to dream up and achieve their highest intentions without internal or external limits holding them back. They can bake infinite pies, live their best lives, and make life better for others. It's a virtuous circle. But watch out for those pesky demons.

EXERCISE

Here's a journaling practice that will build your awareness of the power of the infinite pie. Each day for a month, simply ask someone, "How can I help you?" and "How can you help me?" Whatever the answers note them in your journal, including the person you were speaking with. At the end of the month, review the journal and observe what happened as a result. You'll also have created a network you can continue to build upon.

9 Power Demons
- Baking small pies
- Not being forward-thinking

- Communicating poorly
- Lacking energy and enthusiasm
- Working 24/7, leaving no time for sharing your pies (or your recipe)
- Being satisfied with the status quo
- Not being open to input from others
- Not asking for help
- Withdrawing from community

INTENTIONAL WOMAN

Dr. Nancy O'Reilly, Clinical Psychologist, Author, Philanthropist, Founder of Women Connect 4 Good Foundation

When I asked Nancy if there was ever a time when she was discouraged about whether she could achieve her intention, she replied, "When I was working on my doctorate, there were 8 of us women in the program and we called ourselves the psych sisters. When one of us thought we weren't going to make it, we always had the support of the others. So many people dropped out of the program—their names would suddenly be gone from their mailboxes—but because we had each other's support, we were able to make it through."

Now, as a philanthropist, Nancy says that it's important for women to be building and "intentioning" their wealth not just to be able help other women individually but to advance women's equality in society overall. She started Women Connect 4 Good because she had felt so often that she didn't have a voice and, like Minda Harts, she wanted to use what she had learned to help other women.

"There is something amazing when a woman helps another woman," she says. "Every single day, lift another woman up. It can be small or big."

You can download Dr. Nancy's *The Lift List* at https://www. drnancyoreilly.com/lwu/ [70] and "arm yourself with 52 weeks of simple actions that will help you step into your power, increase your impact, and build an environment where every person is valued, respected, and equally compensated. Our action goes further together."[71]

INTENTIONAL WOMAN

Entrepreneur, Author, and Million-Dollar Women Coach Julie Pimsleur on the Infinite Pie

Julia Pimsleur built Little Pim from scratch into a multimillion-dollar business teaching languages to young children. She says she benefitted from mentors who helped her get to the next level, including raising $6 million in capital for Little Pim. She knew she didn't have to do it all alone, that if she had the courage to start, she could get support. Two defining moments helped her: The first was hearing the words, "Lift from where you stand," by Warren Rustand, entrepreneur and educator. The second and equally powerful motivation to find the courage was getting incensed about something and joining with others to rectify the injustice.

At film school in France in her early twenties, Julia and a fellow filmmaker were concerned about female genital mutilation (FGM) being performed on African girls in France, with many of these girls being rushed to the hospital from blood loss. So they created a film to show the dangers. The film earned a French Human Rights Award, was broadcast on TV, and served as material at the International Gathering of Women in Dakar, where thousands protested against FGM using the film in their staging. What she learned from this was, "Never underestimate the power of a few people working together to change the world." Julia's statement parallels a quote from the late famed anthropologist Margaret Mead, who said, "Never doubt that a small group of thoughtful committed citizens can change the world. Indeed, it's the only thing that ever has."

After turning Little Pim into a global language-teaching powerhouse, Julia wrote her book, *Million Dollar Women*,[72] which didn't just focus on her own company's success; it featured other women who had taken their businesses past the million-dollar-per-year milestone as well.

These days, Julia is devoting her full energy to the Million Dollar Women organization, a thriving social venture that has continually multiplied its resources for women entrepreneurs. Talk about infinite pie! The organization's mission is to get over one million women to reach $1 million in yearly revenue for their businesses. They do this via their four-month online business school for women called Million Dollar Women Masterclass, as well as through the Million Dollar Mind podcast that she hosts, the Million Dollar Women Summit, and a nonprofit scholarship program for women of color entrepreneurs. Presently she is building the Million Dollar Coach Certification program, sure to expand the pie even further.

If in her early twenties, while in film school in a foreign country, Julia hadn't become incensed about an injustice she saw perpetrated against young girls, who knows if her intentioning would have been put toward a different purpose. But one thing is for sure: Julia Pimsleur never bakes small pies.

Dr. Nancy gets the last word, with which I wholeheartedly agree: "I believe the year ahead will be a landmark time for women as we redefine our roles and adjust to the post-COVID world. A new modern woman will emerge, and if we work together to #LiftWomenUp, there will be nothing to stop us from achieving anything we put our minds to!"

The pie of opportunity is truly infinite.

THE COUNTERINTUITIVE LEADERSHIP
INTENTIONING TOOLS

Leadership Intentioning Tool #4: Modulate Confidence . . . because self-doubt can have a positive value.

> *"When you face rejection or critical feedback, don't let it get to you. Sometimes it can be quite helpful. It can lead you to an aha. And sometimes, it is invalid, and you ignore it. Too often, women get downtrodden when they face rejection—but it's the only way you can grow as a leader."*—DEBRA STERLING, FOUNDER OF GOLDIEBLOX

There's a whole industry telling women they need more confidence as though it's something you can inject into your veins like a COVID vaccine. But I think confidence is overrated. Yes, you need to feel comfortable in your own skin. Yes, you need to have the skills and the will to go about intentioning in your daily life without second-guessing yourself.

But self-doubt can have a positive value. You would never get better at anything if you thought you were already perfect. Dissatisfied people are more likely to create and innovate to solve problems. The trick is not to be immobilized by self-doubt but to turn it into positive analysis and solutions. And to give yourself well-deserved affirmations when you succeed.

Here is a different take on making *mistake*s. Everyone knows what the word means, but have you thought about the feelings that stir around the term "mistakes"? The paralyzing self doubt sucking the air out of your actions, and your intentioning, whether you fear a first mistake or you made a mistake and fear making more. Do you obsess about mistakes you have made, usurping your confidence?

If you haven't ever screwed up, believe me, you aren't learning. You're not taking risks that enable you to grow and thrive. You're missing opportunities to innovate. Self-doubt in the search for absolute confidence can freeze your ability to act, but if used in a positive way, it can support the quality of your intentioning practice.

Notable accidental life-saving innovations, which might have been called mistakes at the start, have included penicillin and the pacemaker. Life-changing accidental innovations include potato chips, bubble wrap, and the microwave. Embrace those mistakes. Yours might just save the world. Be open to that fortuity. Intentioning doesn't mean that you control every result. It does mean that you know your intention and don't let the quest for perfection keep you from taking the actions necessary to achieve it.

....

It never occurred to me that I could be a CEO because I had never seen a woman in that role.

....

When I was growing up in rural West Texas, if a woman wanted or, heaven forbid, needed to work, she had three options: to become a teacher, a nurse, or a secretary. So when I started attending college after my third child was born, I figured I would become a teacher since I had done poorly in typing in high school and I couldn't stand the sight of blood.

It never crossed my mind that I could run anything larger than a classroom until the departing executive director asked me to interview at Planned Parenthood in West Texas, after I had met her only once when interviewing her for a term paper in my ecology class—the last class I took before finally, after a twelve-year effort, finishing my degree. I expected to do my student teaching that fall and then spend the rest of my career as a high school social studies teacher. Lo and behold, when much to my surprise I was offered and accepted the job as CEO of that affiliate, I discovered I have what I call the "CEO brain." However, that didn't keep me from breaking out in hives daily for the first month because of lack of confidence—after all, I had never run an organization, knew nothing about health care administration, and knew only what I had learned while doing my term paper about the reproductive rights movement.

For me, the CEO brain means that you will take on a high level of responsibility in order to have the opportunity to make things happen. I found I was able to have a vision and bring resources together to execute it. I was intentioning for a cause I believed in.

The crazy part is that I would have never known I had these qualities if I hadn't said "yes" to an opportunity for which I was not 100 percent, maybe not even 25 percent, prepared. But precisely because I lacked confidence, I worked very hard, learned everything I could about what I didn't know, and sought advice from volunteers and staff alike. Here's a secret: I actually think I have done my best work in every job I've had because I didn't already know it all before I started.

You, too, have the capacity to do more than you can imagine if you don't wait till you have that elusive thing called confidence. I guarantee you that a man would put his hat in the ring whether or not he thought he was 100 percent qualified. It's also interesting to note that about 70 percent of both men and women claim to have imposter syndrome. But men go ahead and take action anyway, whereas women are more likely to second-guess themselves and stand back from the action.

The worst that can happen is that you take the action, it doesn't turn out well, and you return to your original plan. Or you have learned something, made new contacts, and a different opportunity in line with your intention comes your way. What seems like a failure can open new doors and give us the power to start a new chapter, better than we ever imagined.

INTENTIONAL WOMAN

Losing Steam but Following Her Heart Won the Day for Bianca Caban

I met Bianca Caban when we were both speaking at a very disorganized conference in Brooklyn in 2018 and had been sent to a holding room to await our turns on the stage. I was immediately taken by her energy and asked if I could interview her for this book.

Born in the Bronx of Puerto Rican descent, Bianca had been in a program called Better Chance that helped low-income kids get into top schools. She attended Harvard where several events set her intentions toward using the power of the financial industry to bring more prosperity to all women and especially women of color. First, she interned at the Women's Center. She calls that experience "transformational" as it opened her eyes to women's empowerment. Second, hearing sexist comments about how women are inherently not adept at science and engineering, made by the then-president of Harvard, Lawrence Summers, further elevated her awareness of the gender discrimination that is so deeply rooted in our culture. Soon thereafter, she noticed that Latinas didn't have a significant voice on campus, so she decided to do her social activism class project on developing the Harvard College Latina Empowerment and Development Conference.

Bianca earned her MBA at Columbia, started a consultancy, and while trying to understand how to get more capital to people of color, she learned about equity crowdfunding and impact investing. Another lightbulb moment occurred: "Oh," she said, "you can use capital for good!" A client led her to Republic, a private investing platform with a startup crowdfunding model, where she became Director of Partnerships. She was able to apply what she had learned previously, which is: *When you invest in women, they tend to reinvest in their families globally*. She realized that investing in women as a tool of business growth grows the whole economy.

I caught up with her early in 2021 to find out how the pandemic had affected her. She'd had a baby and, like all of us, was working from home. She's now a principal at another investing firm, Heartland, a position she took in the midst of the pandemic, and her personal intention hasn't changed. But she acknowledged that when she was in the throes of her entrepreneurial journey, going through her personal and family savings to build her business, there were many times when she felt like she wasn't getting traction. She lost confidence, lost steam, and at one point asked herself, "Man, can this really work?"

But she followed her heart. One day after a meeting that didn't go well, she got a call from a reporter at *Cosmopolitan* magazine, saying they were giving her their Fun Fearless Latina award. She had been working head down, not seeing any money coming in, and that validation helped teach her that at some point if you keep doing what you believe in, and trust your gut, you will get signs from the universe that will conspire to support you. I assure you she is right.

For me, 30 years after accepting that call to submit a resume for a job I had little confidence in myself to do, I retired as the organization's national president where I had the amazing opportunity to revitalize it, creating a 25-year vision to expand health services and turning it into an advocacy powerhouse. A new energy was breathed into the organization by my intentioning. And now I am able to take all that I learned on that job and other life experiences and share it with you in this book and through Take The Lead! Am I 100 percent confident that we will reach leadership parity by 2025? No, but that's exactly what drives me to find the solutions that will ensure success.

EXERCISE

Paint a mental picture of a time when you felt highly confident and sailed through your work or achieved your goal with only a bit of self-doubt. What were those circumstances? Then paint a mental picture of a time when you lacked confidence to do your work or achieve your goal. What were those circumstances? Compare and contrast the two. What are the feelings and behaviors that you want to bring forward to your next challenge? What will you release to the universe because it doesn't serve you? You may wish to write this in your workbook or journal.

9 Power Demons
- Not celebrating achievements
- Only seeing risk, not reward
- Lacking clarity of mission and vision
- Aiming for perfection

- Needing your comfort zone more than your goal
- Suffering from imposter syndrome
- Avoiding conflict
- Intimidating rather than inspiring
- Being self-centered, looking only inward

INTENTIONAL WOMAN

Heli Rodriguez Prilliman, Founder and CEO of Lacquerbar, on Modulating Confidence

"Because beauty school sucked" is her company's tagline. Let's hear it for an intentional woman who says it like it is. Lacquerbar is a venture-backed, consumer, educational, and business-to-business tech startup that successfully raised a $1M series seed round led by Precursor Ventures. Lacquerbar is overhauling the $20 billion antiquated nail salon industry by offering a feminist-focused salon experience that's powered by their elite nail technician education platform, Lacquerbar U.[73]

Part of why I love Heli's story, and shared some of it in chapter 3, is because she thought bigger when challenged and then acted on her intention to execute despite her admitted lack of confidence. You grow those confidence muscles by using them to get ever closer to your intention.

Within her first year of business, with only $200,000 pre-seed funding, Heli built an award-winning nail brand that generated over $400,000 in revenue and received the backing of Founder Gym and Oakland Startup Network.

Heli grew up in a small farming town, an hour southwest of Fort Worth. Her father was an undocumented immigrant from Mexico who got his citizenship and owned a small business. Her mother, whose dad served in the U.S. military, was also Mexican-American. When Heli's father died, her then-single mom still found time to be an activist and march for farm workers' rights even though she was caring for four children at home. Watching her mother take such a stance helped mold who she is today. Heli paid for college through scholarships. She worked in advertising agencies and got laid off twice.

During one of those dry times, Heli took a big risk when a friend of a friend was starting a tech company in the Bay Area. She moved there and became the first female employee at a frat-house-like company in a warehouse building reminiscent of the office in the movie *The Social Network*. These men became Heli's family. Apparently, a tight-enough family for her to stay five and a half years, working in sales, package design, tech management, user experience, content strategy, branding, and marketing.

Throughout the process of helping this company grow, Heli kept saying, "I don't ever want to have my own company!" Never say never ... or don't ever!

The idea for Lacquerbar came, as so often happens, from her personal experience and passion. Getting her nails done was a luxury, and many of the nail salon environments, even with the increasing popularity of girls' weekends, didn't feel very luxurious unless they were expensive. Those salons offering wine and champagne did, perhaps, but they weren't necessarily a fun environment, and they didn't offer nail art or any of the other emerging quality nail techniques. Maybe it's the Texan in her, she says, but Heli likes to get her nails done and have a margarita! She wanted to go to an experiential place that was also feminist-focused. The defining moment came when she decided to build her own multi-faceted nail business that would disrupt the industry.

She raised $100,000 in angel investment money and then took out a $100,000 small business loan to open the first location in Berkeley, California. She left her job and enrolled in beauty school so she could understand what it was like to be a beauty technician. This drove her level of intentioning up. "I found the education system for nail tech and salon workers is very predatory and antiquated, teaching you things from the '90s." It disappointed her that they didn't teach students how to be successful or to make money.

"They tell you to be your own boss! Have your own studio! The reality is that you're lucky to get out of beauty school to make $9 an hour." Beauty school, according to Heli, can cost anywhere from $5,000 to $40,000. She said to pay for the tuition many of these schools help students take out grants, but they also accept credit cards. Because so many women of color and from foreign countries attend these schools, Heli was concerned by how much debt they incurred. "They don't have all the business insight to get out of that debt. It's just a horrible cycle of poverty," she told me.

So she set out to teach nail technicians from scratch, even if they had been to outdated schools before attending her program. The process entailed a week of training to determine if they could swing it. That didn't go so well; they experienced high turnover and were burning through money to conduct the training. That pushed Heli to start an online education center, which, as she said, "Nail technicians everywhere are begging for."

To give me an idea of the expense involved she told me that to open a Dry Bar in the Bay Area typically costs about $700,000. "I raised $200,000," she said. "I was still able to build this online brand and we are known throughout the country for amazing nail art and drinks. It's also women's empowerment."

She had to take out small loans here and there. Her husband and even her parents helped out with a thousand dollars to start and then a thousand dollars to keep things afloat. "I'm not the typical start-up founder: a white or Asian male who went to Harvard or works at Goldman Sachs, previous Google employee, or anything like that. I didn't have the network of wealth that some people do for venture capital. It's all about warm introductions to raise investment money. If you get an introduction from someone you know or trust, you get an email, [that's] where it may start."

Can you relate? Heli had setbacks and power demons that wanted to tell her the dream was too audacious. People or investors would drag her along, but they didn't get her vision. Most of them were men who had not been exposed to people who have gone to beauty school. They didn't think there would be much money in it. Needless to say, Heli endured a lot of "mansplaining." She ultimately found ways to get her vision across without spending so much time answering questions about beauty trends and culture.

I have confidence that Heli will persevere, and I look forward to seeing what she does with Lacquerbar once we are fully out of the pandemic. I can't wait to get a mani, pedi, and enjoy a margarita with her.

Three Tips to Help You Modulate Confidence with Positive Intention

1. The first tip is don't stay small and don't play small. Look outward at what the world might need instead of inward at your own lack of confidence. Waiting to become totally confident is like waiting for Godot. It'll never happen. That's why I say confidence is overrated. Always leave room for a measure of healthy doubt about your ability so that you will have the humility to keep learning.

   I realize that can be hard to do when you are dealing with a complex situation and you want everything to be perfect. Many of us have that perfection impulse, especially women because we have been socialized and rewarded for looking and performing perfectly. So we try to make everything we do at home and at work flawless.

   And it's also true that from early career up to the C suite, women in leadership often are judged more harshly when they don't meet that perfection standard or when they make what is considered a mistake. That can affect your upward mobility if you accept being judged at face value.

   But how many men have you seen fail upward? In other words, how often have you seen men who have been fired brazenly ask for and quickly be thrown a lifeline in the form of another and sometimes even higher position by another male? Boys learn from an early age to play competitive games where there are winners and losers, and everyone comes back to play another day. There is a culture of helping one another. And women are finally learning the inestimable value of mutual support too.

2. My second tip for modulating confidence is know that sometimes faster is better than better. Sometimes 80 or 90 percent of a plan done is better than getting 100 percent of it perfected on the drawing board. You can always improve it later in the execution.

   I know that in the new reality many of us are facing it is easy to be overcome with fear about the future and to resist taking risks. And it's challenging to maintain those all-important relationships when we are working from home day after day.

3. So my third tip is quite simply not to lose sight of your purpose. Stay focused on the vision you are intentioning into being. No matter how difficult and challenging times are now—they will get better. Resist the temptation to make everyone happy all the time, especially when going through a rough patch in an organization or in your life. It takes a strong leader to nurture and guide disparate stakeholders to coalesce around a vision that remains true to the mission, even as strategies for advancing the mission may change over time due to changes in the marketplace, technology, or funding sources.

   It's essential to get to extreme clarity, to know when you would walk away, or risk being fired rather than violate those values. Clarity of vision is more liberating than confidence. It frees you to do a better job because it gives you the power to show up in your integrity. And most of the time, you discover that people follow people with integrity, courage, and a clear point of view.

   Power and energy come from projecting into new spaces, not from standing still waiting until you are confidently ready. Every perceived threat or setback can become an opportunity to find a new way to serve your purpose. Paradoxically, just as when you seek happiness for its own sake you are unlikely to find it, when you modulate confidence and don't let its absence keep you from taking action, you will by virtue of your action become more confident in your ability to achieve your intention.

Leadership Intentioning Tool #5: Strike Your Own Damn Balance (and Love Your Stress) . . . because ultimately you get to choose what matters to you and unchoose the rest. Pay no attention to the man behind the curtain telling you you're supposed to be unhappy.

> *"I've never been a white-water-raftin', bungee-jumpin' kind of girl—that's not how I define adventure for myself. What I know for sure is this: The most important journey of our lives doesn't necessarily involve climbing the highest peak or trekking around the world. The biggest adventure you can ever take is to live the life of your dreams."*
> —OPRAH WINFREY

The title of this chapter might make you think that I'm going to make your life easier. It's actually going to help you do one of the hardest things in life—decide what you will and won't be intentioning in your one precious lifetime. That's not necessarily easy but it is most definitely necessary if you are going to be an intentional woman. And that will lead you to ease and joy.

Ultimately, you have to choose what matters to you and unchoose the rest. Be prepared to hear me say radical things such as: Put parenthood on your resume. Define beauty on your own terms. Love your stress. Don't go with someone else's version of "balance" in this life—it's as impossible and empty as someone else's version of success or perfection. The colors on your palette are yours, for good or ill.

Once you have uncovered yourself, you will be able to detect if your life choices are coming from the authentic you or from external forces that don't necessarily have your best interests at heart.

Every choice requires us to give up what we didn't choose. Choice is sacrifice as well as freedom. But we can always unchoose as deliberately as we chose, and then choose another intention. Persistence is key. You have walked through the door, now what? You are in a position of power to choose, what will you do?

Which of the big five are most important to you? Money, power, status, quality of life, enjoyment of what you do? What's least important? Do you know? If you have multiple ambitions, are you aware of what your priorities are? Are you wringing your hands about your choices because someone said along the way, "You can't have it all?" Well, I am here to tell you that you can have all that you truly want—all that you set about intentioning. Even if you don't get it all at one time or all the time, you can have all that you intention.

The original title of this interesting study is all in caps, not just because of my desire to emphasize the words: STUDY SHOWS SUCCESSFUL, AMBITIOUS PEOPLE REALLY DO HAVE IT ALL. It began in 1922, almost a century ago, when psychologist Lewis Terman of Stanford began studying more than 1,500 highly intelligent children in California. Over the next 70 years, the participants were asked about their activity patterns, vocational histories, emotional development, home life, and other data. In 2012, Timothy Judge of the University of Notre Dame and John D. Kammeyer-Mueller of the Warrington College of Business sorted through this data. They found that ambitious people who achieved their life's goals lived longer than ambitious people who hadn't.[74]

"I guess you could say that those people got it all," said Judge. I would prefer to think they were reaping the energizing and mental health benefits of intentioning.

That phrase "have it all" is likely most questioned by parents, especially mothers who still bear more than their share of child-care responsibilities. After all, kids may be our greatest joy in life, but parenting takes a great deal of time and other resources physically, mentally, emotionally, and financially. There are infinite experiences to be had, lessons to be learned, and growth to be endured both for child *and* parent.

Women are told over and over that they can't possibly have it all, most likely by those who don't want them to succeed as leaders, or to have equal power in society. Because are men ever told this?

When I facilitated a panel on negotiation at the Watermark Lead on Conference for Women[75] in Silicon Valley, the room was packed with all chairs filled and women leaning two deep along every wall, eager to learn useful tips to get paid and promoted fairly. They started lining up for the mic well before the panelists had finished speaking. There was no way we could get to all of their brightly burning questions.

It was my job to call time, but I decided to take one more question from a woman who looked to be around 40 years old, energetically pleading for a chance to get the panel's response. "I have a master's in engineering," she said, "and worked in increasingly responsible positions in tech companies for fifteen years. I opted to take a few years off to be with my children, and now I can't get back anywhere near the career path I was on when I left. I've tried to stay up to date, but hiring people focus on the employment gap in my resume. What should I do?"

Now, I have three children. Nothing I have done—not teaching school, not writing books, not even being president and CEO of a huge national organization or starting a new nonprofit—has taught me as much as raising those kids. Organizational skills, budgeting, juggling multiple priorities, communication skills, dealing with diverse personalities, crisis management, developing innovative solutions to seemingly intractable problems—you name it, parents do it.

Before throwing the question to the negotiation experts on the panel, I blurted out, "Put parenthood on your resume and list the skills you have learned from it, the things you have accomplished because of it."

Cheers erupted. I think it's because the women in the room all know it's an idea whose time has come. It is a core seed of striking your own balance. And we have allies we probably aren't calling upon to the fullest.

In June 2019, Pew Research Center unveiled findings on fathers taking more active roles in their children's lives and around the house while navigating demands of work and family. That this line of research even exists—and more frequently is public discourse—is promising since the bulk of narrative concerning work-life balance in the past was solely focused on women. Pew discovered:[76]

- *More dads are staying home to care for their kids.* Dads made up 17 percent of all stay-at-home parents in 2016, up from 10 percent in 1989.
- *Dads see parenting as central to their identity.* Dads are just as likely as moms to say that parenting is extremely important to their identity. Some 57 percent of fathers said this compared to 58 percent of mothers.
- *Work-family balance is a challenge for many working fathers.* Just like mothers, many of today's fathers find it challenging to balance work and family life. About half of working dads (52 percent) said in 2015 that it is very or somewhat difficult to do so, a slightly smaller share than the 60 percent of working mothers who said the same. My son has acknowledged that he chose not to put himself forward for certain advancement opportunities for the sake of being an actively engaged father and not uprooting his family.

Power sharing in the home is still not on parity, and as we have seen, the burdens on women have become much more unbalanced due to the pressures of COVID—home schooling and other care-giving responsibilities. But I suggest that this heightened attention to the disparity has raised awareness of the need for a national child-care policy that allows both genders to work outside the home. This can be turned into a key opportunity for normalizing a more egalitarian culture. As Gloria Steinem has observed, democracy begins in the home.

Now, living in the dual pandemics of coronavirus and racial injustices laid bare for over a year is taking its toll on even the most naturally optimistic and flexible of us. Many are feeling loss of control. Loss of human contact. Perhaps loss of jobs or income, and even loss of the life of someone near and dear.

Pent-up fury at the murders of Black men and women by those deputized to protect and defend us. Frustration with changes in routines we had adapted to and concerns about what a return to our offices will mean for our health, productivity, and for our planet's climate. This is a very hard time. Make no mistake about that.

INTENTIONAL WOMAN

Striking Her Own Balance, Award-Winning Journalist Soledad O'Brien Focuses Her Energy on Creating the Career of Her Choice

I recently had the opportunity to interview one of the television journalists I most admire, Soledad O'Brien, [77] when she generously joined me in a Zoom fireside chat, to which I had invited both our 2019 and 2020 cohorts of 50 Women Can Change the World in Journalism.[78]

Soledad is an Emmy and Peabody award winner and executive producer. She has struck her own balance as the host of *Matter of Fact with Soledad O'Brien*, a nationally syndicated weekly talk show produced by Hearst Television, and has previously worked with several major networks including NBC, MSNBC, and CNN, coanchoring the latter's *American Morning* program. I was fortunate to be interviewed by her a few times in those roles.

So it was a special pleasure to turn the tables and ask Soledad about how she founded and helms Soledad O'Brien Productions, her multiplatform media production and distribution company,[79] and more specifically, about how she has been able to create her career with such intentionality.

Like all of us, she was working from home, at her dining room table. She fussed at first about whether the blouse she was wearing was too colorful and I said that given the times we are in, nothing could be too colorful. She shared that in her personal pandemic life, having four older children was a gift because each one of them could help with her work and family chores.

Soledad is a mosaic of America. She is the daughter of two immigrants. Her father, who is white, is from Australia and is of Irish and Scottish heritage; her mother is Afro-Cuban. I noticed during our conversation that she referred frequently to how she had used her energy, especially in response to questions about how she had gained the courage to thrive even in newsrooms where racism and sexism were prevalent. She said that a great deal of her focus on combating racism had started when she was asked to host CNN's series *Black in America.*[80] She noticed that individuals of color were described based on their deficits whereas suburban whites were described by focusing first on their assets and agency.

But there was a more personal event that occurred early in her career that made her realize how she was wasting energy when she let negative comments deter her from her own intentions.

She relayed that when she worked in local news at WBZ in Boston, she had to attend a regular morning meeting. It started at 7:00 a.m., but she did the show that was on before the *TODAY* show. She was an associate producer, and her show would end just as the 7:00 a.m. meeting started. She would leave the show, exit the control room, run to the bathroom, and arrive at the morning meeting around 7:05. "So I was late every day because I was doing the show," she said. "And there was a guy in my meeting who used to make cracks about, 'Oh, Soledad's running on colored people's time.' I'd go home and I'd think, 'When he says that, here's what I'm gonna say. He's gonna do this and I'm gonna do that.' I spent so much time thinking about this guy. Do you know how much psychic energy I put into that bull? *So* much."

Then she added something that is a great takeaway for all of us. She said, "I tell people, 'Don't do what I did. Focus on growing your career. Focus on opportunities. Focus on staying late, making your writing better, making your reporting better. Focus on getting to know your boss. Focus on understanding how did that person get hired? What skills do you need for this? Don't focus on those stupid, catty, racist, unpleasant, dopey things, misogynistic things that people say.'

"What a waste of energy," she emphasized. "You have to really make sure that you're protecting your psychic energy and working on projects that will grow you, and not getting stuck in those things that suck you under."

Powerful advice! So don't let these Power Demons derail you.

9 Power Demons
- Internal conflict
- Ambiguity about your intention
- Lacking self-awareness
- Laying or shouldering blame
- Suffering burnout
- Lacking follow-through or follow-up
- Exhaustion
- Wasting energy on people and things that don't advance your intention
- Incurring stress related health problems

INTENTIONAL WOMAN

Tiffany Dufu Willingly Drops the Ball

I'm convinced the idea of #worklifebalance is a narrative created to keep women unhappy with their work and therefore to lower their intentions for leadership. It was never a "thing" until women entered the workforce in large numbers. What man has ever been expected to worry about work-life balance? It's another cultural trope stemming from implicit bias. Perhaps not deliberate but just as insidious.

As I tend to say frequently, life presents a series of choices to everyone. You decide what your balance is. When you love and find purpose in your work, it's always fun, even if it's hard or stressful. My work and play have always been fun by intention. I say, strike your own damn balance and pay no attention to the man behind the curtain telling you you're supposed to be unhappy.

Tiffany is a catalyst-at-large in the world of women's leadership. She's the author of *Drop the Ball*, a memoir and manifesto that shows women how to cultivate the skill they need in order to thrive: the ability to let go.[81] She is also the founder and CEO of The Cru, a peer coaching platform for women looking to accelerate their professional and personal growth.

Named to *Fast Company*'s League of Extraordinary Women, Tiffany was a launch team member of Lean In and was Chief Leadership Officer at Levo, a Millennial professional network that no longer exists.[82] Prior to that, Tiffany served as President of The White House Project, as a Major Gifts Officer at Simmons College in Boston, and as Associate Director of Development at Seattle Girls' School.

When you meet her or hear her talk, what you notice first is her radiance, her passion. It's like a spotlight has been powered on. She epitomizes the Intentioning Power Tool of Strike Your Own Balance.

She knows her history and shares it freely. She credits her mother for her confidence. Tiffany's mom felt that her two daughters needed a strong sense of self. She was very intentional about making Tiffany and her sister feel like their opinion mattered. They had to be respectful, but she always found ways for them to share what they thought about things. She was particular about helping other people understand how to interact with the girls in the most effective way versus expecting her daughters to shape and twist themselves to fit someone else's agenda.

Tiffany recounts her first day of kindergarten, an intensely powerful moment. When her mother came to pick her up, her mom overheard her teacher telling Tiffany that she was not a good listener. Tiffany was devastated because she felt she was a good girl, following all the rules. Her mother queried the teacher, "What did you tell Tiffany to do that she shouldn't do?" The teacher replied, "I asked Tiffany to sit down and she didn't."

Now, as a parent, the usual response is to turn to the child and ask why they didn't sit down. Her mother asked, "How did you ask Tiffany to sit down?" The teacher said, "I just asked her to sit down." That wasn't good enough for Tiffany's mom, who engaged the teacher in a role play. She discovered the teacher said, "Tiffany, would you like to sit down?" Her mom looked at the teacher and said, "There's the problem. In my house, I give my children a direct command and Tiffany always listens. You implied that she *may* not want to sit down, and you were giving her the choice and power."

That small but significant role play made Tiffany feel as if she had power and influence. As she moved about in the world, she was able to see that not every challenge she'd encounter would be because of something she did wrong. It may just be that the other person does not quite understand how to interact with Tiffany. Her mother didn't hold judgment against the teacher. She had empathy. And Tiffany didn't have to feel as if she did something wrong. They had just "miscommunicated."

Tiffany's parents were from Watts, a neighborhood in Los Angeles, where Tiffany was conceived in the mid-1970s, a rough time. Her mom encouraged her dad to join the military. That's how Tiffany was born at an U.S. Army base in Tacoma, Washington. Her mother gave up a scholarship to UCLA and became pregnant at 19. Her father attended college on the GI Bill and eventually earned a Ph.D. in theology. He was a preacher and a counselor, a beacon in the community.

Tiffany grew up in a house with a white picket fence around it, not understanding the cycle of poverty, addiction, and violence her parents had managed to obliterate in just one generation. This demonstrates her mother's intentionality around curating a different experience for her children. She used to tell them, "You're so smart, beautiful, and loved." Tiffany explains, "When

I'm around 500 people or whatever the venue, this little voice starts ringing in my head: 'Tiffany, you are so smart. Loved. Beautiful.'"

I wanted to explore the topic of Black women's relationship with power in conversation with Tiffany as a consideration for striking your own balance.

"Yes, this played a role in a positive way," she said. "And yes, in a negative way." To address both, she explained, "I always assumed I had a certain level of power and was powerful. I chose my husband, in part, because he has an African mother. He's from Ghana. I made that assumption: Well, he has an African mother, so he can handle me. I grew up in a very Afro-centric home in which Black women very much represent power, prowess, and firm grounding. I think the way in which that has been a challenge is sometimes there is an expectation for this strength, when sometimes it's not the healthiest response to tragedy. It's okay to be weak. Or crumble or cry. Or not hold yourself up or hold up others. Sometimes."

Tiffany meets so many women every day who didn't have the type of mother she had or even someone else in their lives who consistently told them they are valuable and worthy.

She observes that the way to create more intention around your career and life at its core is often rooted in a sense of adequacy about what you can actually do in the world. The Cru creates tribes of women who fill that gap and encourage their cohort members to understand they can think big *and* be big.

Back in the day when we were able to be with large groups in person for celebratory events, I often saw Tiffany bringing her daughter, even if there were no other children present. This was very intentional. We discussed gendered socialization. She described an "experiment" she conducted with her son and daughter. "Last year, my son, 10, was reading one of those *TIME* ... kid magazines. He needed help with the word, *potential*. Potential: The capacity to improve. I said, 'Do you have potential?' He said, 'No.' I said, 'Potential has the ability to get better. Let me explain another way.' He said, 'I understand what it is. You don't have to explain again ....' Okay. 'So, son, why are you saying you don't have potential?' He looked at me with this big grin and said, 'It doesn't get any better than this!'

"I just laughed. That is it. This is the kid who will have the big idea and change the world. My daughter will need to know this, too, but I have to cultivate this in her because it doesn't come naturally. If I could give one tip, round up! Round up what you think you could do, or what you think your vision could be. You're far more qualified than the guy next to you, yet he's the one in the mirror thinking, *it's mine.*"

The White House Project, a nonprofit that worked to increase representation in U.S. institutions, businesses, and government, closed down while Tiffany was the CEO. It wasn't just that she was shutting down a prominent organization that devastated her; she was doing so to something passed on to her by a mentor, Marie Wilson. "It was like she was handing over her baby and I was letting it die under my watch," Tiffany explains. "The guilt I felt for that was enormous.

"My ability to recover from that experience was connected to a couple of things .... The first was when I was on a beach in Brazil. I was happy with my body but I'd had two babies. I remembered that my daughter had asked me, 'Mommy, why does your tummy look like scrambled eggs?' My head just went into my hands and I started bawling. As I cried, I started to separate my hands and look down. This voice in my head said, *Seriously, Tiffany? Look at every inch of yourself. You're drop-dead gorgeous. The only thing that proves you're a real woman is your tummy. It's your street cred.*

"On the beach, thinking about The White House project, that is what came to me: street cred. Tiffany, you talk about women's leadership, but what street cred do you have as a leader? I'm risk-averse and would rather learn from someone else having gone through something. I've tried hard to curate my path to make it as easy as possible, but The White House Project taught me that easy is not the path to success. I could no longer curate experiences that prevent myself from experiencing the hard part. The hard part gives you substance. The hard part is something to share in story with others. Without struggle, there is no progress."

And there is certainly struggle in striking your own balance. But there is also the mark of success. For Tiffany, it is emphatically what she gives back to her community. At every school from which she has graduated, somewhere on that campus is a plaque that has her name on it, indicating that she did her part. She already knows what will be on her tombstone, her intention: "She got to as many women as she could."

Leadership Intentioning Tool #6: Build Social Capital First . . . because relationships are everything and will ultimately help you as much as educational qualifications or work experience.

> *The world turns on human connections, human connections.*
> —GLORIA FELDT

Yes, I am shamelessly quoting myself. Relationships are everything and will ultimately help you as much as educational qualifications or work experience. This thinking removes the transactional nature of human relationships that may be uncomfortable for women. It enables us to be more authentic and secure in our skins. People follow people who are real and genuine.

I also suggest getting a tandem partner, the metaphor being how skydivers jump in pairs. Get a professional partner who you can call when you are about to jump, who can be objective and understands your struggle, your SIS (sister in strength). Return the favor often.

I had long admired Nina Vaca from her reputation and from following each other on social media. I had the opportunity to interview her virtually for a webchat on entrepreneurship[83] a few years ago. I finally met her in person when we both spoke at a conference in New York.

Nina is a ninja at building social capital. Her first rule for business and life is: Be crazy good. Simple and sweet! Nina is the Chairman and CEO of Pinnacle Group, a Dallas-based workforce solutions provider. She has led the company forward, transforming it into the workforce solutions powerhouse it is today, offering a suite of business lines that address workforce challenges faced by companies all over the world. In addition to her business pursuits, Nina's connectivity includes being a philanthropist and civic leader. She is a staunch advocate for female entrepreneurs, especially within the Hispanic and minority communities. Nina was appointed a Presidential Ambassador for Global

Entrepreneurship by President Barack Obama. She's received three honorary doctorates and is the youngest distinguished alumna in Texas State University history. Yep, another Texan showing up as an intentioner! What she's not is an isolated, do-it-alone kind of person.

She told *CEOWORLD Magazine,* when asked to give advice to women starting out as entrepreneurs, the space where social capital is everything. "I'm a firm believer in teams and large support networks. No human is an island, and I would advise anyone to build a team of individuals that genuinely wants to see you succeed. This also means expanding networks to include sponsors, advisors, collaborators, and supporters. This is closely related to my belief that relationships are crucial for business success. Having a support network of individuals around who want the best for you isn't the only ingredient for success, but it's nearly impossible without it."[84]

EXERCISE

Make your Power Map. You can download this exercise at www.intentioningbook.com or simply draw on a sheet of paper. Start with a circle in the center and into it put the name of the person who has the most control over your career trajectory. Next, draw a separate circle and put into it where you sit in relation to that person—next to her or farther away. Continue to name other circles in relation to where they are to the person in that center circle and to you. Now you will be able to analyze those connections, see visually which relationships you need to spend more time cultivating, and set intentions about doing that.

9 Power Demons
- Loneliness
- Resistance to adopting new tools for community and engagement
- Distance from collaboration
- Lack of integrity

- Having to win at all costs
- Focusing on "otherness" instead of unifying thoughts and ideas
- Domination
- Hostility and aggression
- Bullying

INTENTIONAL WOMAN

Publicity Powerhouse and Connector Selena Soo on Building Social Capital

Selena Soo specializes in publicity and marketing strategy. This already tells me that she is all about building social capital. After all, publicity is based on reaching out to the public and cultivating relationships to develop presence as it relates to interpersonal skills.

Selena discussed the motivation behind her business with Celinne Da Costa for *Forbes*:[85] "Growing up in a wealthy community in Hong Kong, I became aware of the power of relationships and the value of nurturing them, even as a little girl. My dad was a successful stockbroker and entrepreneur who regularly hosted dinner parties at our home to build relationships with clients. I learned many lessons about wealth, business, and connection just by attending these gatherings. Years later, I moved to New York City for college on a temporary student visa. I desperately wanted to stay in the U.S., but I was automatically disqualified from most jobs because companies didn't want to sponsor an entry-level employee for a visa. While I felt like I had no control over my future, these doors shutting in front of me lit a fire to become a person who opens doors for others."

Early on, Selena garnered testimonials from key people and worked hard to strengthen those relationships first. Soon she blossomed into a publicity and marketing strategist who helps experts, authors, and coaches go from "hidden gem" to admired industry leader (and even household names). She's helped clients and students get featured in places such as *O, The Oprah Magazine, Forbes,* and *Inc.*, and land interviews on popular podcasts and national TV. Many of Selena's clients have become industry leaders with 7-figure businesses, raving fan bases, and hundreds of thousands of followers.

Her signature approach comes down to building powerful and long-lasting relationships with influencers and the media in a thoughtful, authentic way. With that, she created Impacting Millions training to help entrepreneurs get their message out to the universe.[86]

Her *power to* as a "super-connector" gives her the ability to network for connection over transaction and recommends that everyone develop an "influencer list" of people who can help you reach your goals faster through strategic, synergistic relationships—intentional win-win relationships. This is very similar to the Power Map exercise I gave you. If your values don't match, don't have them on your influencer list. And yes, this may require discovery time, not just a quick sip of coffee with our friend, Google!

You would think that I'm describing a world-class extrovert easefully hobnobbing and talking to anyone. Wrong. Selena will candidly tell you that she has always been shy. But she also recognized that courage intensifies with action. Seeing things in your mind as *done* is a signature element of intentioning.

Selena wants all women to build social capital and advises, "Mind who you are surrounded by. Changing your environment to be with people who are successful and inspiring helps you be more inspiring and successful. Get on newsletters of people who are successful, read their books . . . . The environment you set for yourself makes all the difference."

During her company's latest launch, which took place during the height of the COVID-19 disruption, Selena's team adapted messaging to acknowledge the challenges people were going through. "As leaders, it's important to show our audience that we deeply understand their fears, concerns, and dreams," she said. "People are craving more hearted centered, authentic leadership than ever before. They want real and truthful, not perfect. Showing emotion and connecting to people's struggles make you more trustworthy to your audience."

Like I said, the world turns on human connections.

THE SYSTEMS CHANGE LEADERSHIP
INTENTIONING TOOLS

Leadership Intentioning Tool #7: Be Unreasonable

. . . because sometimes you have to break the rules and invent new ones to get where you want to go.

"The reasonable man adapts to the world. The unreasonable
one persists in trying to adapt the world to himself.
Therefore all progress depends on the unreasonable man."
—GEORGE BERNARD SHAW

Yes, yes, I know. But let's give old GBS the benefit of the doubt that if he were living today, he would have included women in this wise and witty quote. After all, what he is suggesting definitely applies to us. Sometimes you have to break the rules and invent new ones to make progress. If you can dream it, you can do it. Think differently—turn the world upside down and assume a different perspective. Care enough to make it happen.

Seeing with different eyes is the first step to sparking innovation and creating solutions to complex problems. For example, I have always found that creating and/or viewing art in its many forms—painting, photography, dance, sculpting, fashion, literature—instantly shakes out the mental cobwebs so I can innovate and solve complex problems. Art builds empathy and enables you to coalesce others around a vision. It's chicken soup for the leader's soul.

Sometimes art can help us be unreasonable in how we approach a topic that we have learned from our culture to see in a normative way. For example, gender. How often do women so very reasonably adapt ourselves to the expectations of how our bodies "should" be? Do you ever ask yourself why? Well, let me describe what happened when art engaged us in a little unreasonable gender adaptation.

At a fundraising event for Take The Lead hosted by artist Linda Stein at her gallery,[87] our guests quickly got into the spirit, transfixed by Stein's over-the-top gorgeous body-swapping sculptures, wall pieces, and wearable art. It was clear that we had entered an entirely different visual culture. Women and men alike were encouraged to don the pieces and draw in their feminine power. Everyone started to see the entire construct of gender differently. The conversation about the mission they had come to support—women's leadership parity—became lighter, more open, and optimistic in an inviting environment. We were feeling it in our bodies.

"Today the most successful companies don't just out-compete their rivals. They redefine the terms of competition by embracing one-of-a-kind ideas in a world of copycat thinking. Which means, almost by definition, that the best leaders see things that other leaders don't see," writes *Fast Company* magazine cofounder Bill Taylor in *Harvard Business Review*. "Art, it turns out, can be an important tool to change how leaders see their work."[88]

Art opens the mind and feeds a leader's soul in a way that allows such unreasonable thoughts into the mind. Empathy is enhanced and that, in turn, draws people together. That's why I routinely include poetry, drawing, and music into our 50 Women Can Change the World programs,[89] to help the participants open their minds to ideas otherwise deemed unreasonable in their journeys to leadership.

These immersive programs are for emerging women leaders in various sectors such as health care, finance, journalism, tech, entrepreneurship, and entertainment. For the most part, the participants don't know one another before they come together. But soon, they form cohorts, learn the infinite pie theory, and are encouraged to uncover themselves to dream up together. Many of the women express fears about their abilities and perceived barriers to career advancement when they start. They benefit by meeting women who are role models in their fields, such as Soledad O'Brien was for our journalism cohort.

INTENTIONAL WOMAN

Charlotte Jorst, Entrepreneur and Horsewoman

You met Charlotte Jorst when I quoted her ideas about risk previously. She is all about risk over reason. Originally from Denmark, she was taught "profit" was a bad word, and this seemed unreasonable to her! At 18, she moved to France and worked in a restaurant and ski resort before returning to Denmark to attend college. She met her then-husband, who worked for Carlsberg beer, and became "Miss Carlsberg."

I would love to plant a chip in every woman in order to replace fear with the ability to be as "unreasonable" as Charlotte is. She shared how this attribute led to her success with *Fortune* writer Dinah Eng in December 2019.[90] "Back then, it was fashionable to give watches to your employees for Christmas. So, while I was traveling as Miss Carlsberg, I started representing a Danish company that sold premium watches that could be customized with a company's logo. Absolut Vodka was my first customer. When I wasn't traveling, I'd walk the streets of New York, pick buildings with names of big corporations, and go looking for marketing managers to sell our watches to. Sometimes I got thrown out, but sometimes they saw me, and it would lead to an order. I wanted to do a watch for the Guggenheim Museum and kept calling the marketing manager. He agreed to see me, but when I walked in, he was so irate. He got within a centimeter of my nose, saying, 'You're so pushy!'

"Two days later, I called him back, and he ended up giving me an order. When he moved to the Whitney, he continued to buy from me. I built the business by continually calling people and being pushy." Or, as some would call it, by being unreasonably intentional.

Charlotte's advice: "Focus in on your strengths, then your weaknesses become less apparent." She and her then-husband started Skagen, a small watch company, which Fossil later bought. And, of course, pursuing her love for riding at the age of 35 and turning it into a competitive career around the world was by all accounts unreasonable too.

She said, "Women need to stop asking for advice when the advice they want is a justification of their idea. They want to be told to go do it, and then they don't do it. The hardest part of a new company is to start it. Just do it and solve the problems as you go. It doesn't have to be a huge idea. Just a new twist. Always a small idea that ends up being a bigger idea. The fear is the problem. I have fears like everyone else. And failures. I was ashamed of failing in a horse show. Everybody has [the] same amount of fears—it's how you overcome them that matters."

Are you noticing a pattern of intentional women advising you to just start? Even when it seems unreasonable? You will be amazed how just beginning with intention feeds into more and more action until you've realized your goal.

After Charlotte developed skin cancer twice, she invented Kastel Denmark, a UV-protective clothing company, whose sales shot up by 30 percent during the pandemic. The company is so popular that she conducts business on the road around her competition schedule.

Ever the unreasonable woman, Charlotte advises all of us intentioners during this uncertain time: "Stay the course and stay informed. There is so much misinformation out there and you have to stay with what can benefit you and your business. You have to take risks even if that means you have to move, not see your kids for a while, be unpopular. You cannot be successful if you are not focused and risk-taking. There are always so many reasons why you cannot or should not do something. They are there to be overcome."

EXERCISE

What is your impossible dream? Your unreasonable intention? Write it, draw it, sing the song that most represents it. Tell it to someone you trust. When you declare your unreasonable intention, you are more likely to do it. Maybe not today, but you will, using your Leadership Intentioning Tools.

9 Power Demons
- Resistance to innovation
- Denying change is occurring or outright avoiding it
- Saturation
- Stagnation
- Burnout
- Choosing technology over people
- Sarcasm
- Self-deprecation
- Division

INTENTIONAL WOMAN

Rupa Dash, Cofounder and CEO Dash Global Media Has a Moon Shot Vision

Rupa Dash became a great friend when she invited me to speak at her World Woman Foundation conference that she held at the Clinton Center in Little Rock, Arkansas. It's hard to get to Little Rock from anywhere, and I wasn't sure I wanted to make the trip. But I was so glad I did because I was wowed by her and her big—and some would say, unreasonable—vision for a better world.

Rupa is an entertainment entrepreneur based in Los Angeles. She is the cofounder and CEO of Dash Global Media, a leading entertainment company focused on film packaging for world cinema. She is also the CEO of World Woman Foundation, heading a global mentorship program for women and their influence on global issues.

An ardent advocate for social entrepreneurship and leadership development for women in business and entertainment, Rupa is the first Indian-American Managing Director of the World's Largest Women Entrepreneurship Network recognized by the White House.

She has worked with Prime Minister Narendra Modi on India's Vibrant Gujarat Global Summit and with Chief Minister Nitish Kumar in a collaboration with the United Kingdom's Department for International Development to bring useful resources to the most underdeveloped states in India. She is also the recipient of the UN's International Telecom Union Award for her work in bringing mobile entertainment content to Indian farmers across 40,000 villages.

World Woman Foundation believes that "*Equality for women is progress for all.*" Their global moon shot—their intrepid mission—is to reimagine the #equalfuture by investing in one million female heroes by 2030. Guided by this mission, WWF is committed to activate and accelerate women's leadership in a bold new way with long-term investments in capacity building, content development and commerce opportunities through STEAM mentorship programs.[91] The timing is right to have a new kind of thinking and redefine women's role as capital catalysts for a thriving economy and a sustainable planet.

I love that Rupa's unreasonable intentioning focus is on unity and equity—and "moon shots"—with a network that is known for thinking and executing in the millions. She is committed to unleashing the power of women to solve humanity's grand challenges. As Dash said at the conference she hosted, "Today, women are the single largest productive economic force and drive almost every economic indicator for businesses. The attendees will gain tools and strategies to get prepared to be the disruptive force on the planet to make a real impact." And during the conference, she unveiled one after another of what she referred to as "moon shots"—specific areas where women could be completely unreasonable and disrupt the status quo to solve humanity's most intractable problems, whether it involves sustainable development, economic advancement, or eradicating food scarcity worldwide.

Rupa was echoing the famous 1962 speech by President John F. Kennedy when he declared that the U.S. would land a man on the moon within the decade. "We choose to go to the moon and do these other things, not because they are easy but because they are hard, because that goal will serve to organize and measure the best of our energies and skills, because that challenge is one that we are willing to accept, one we are unwilling to postpone, and one we intend to win, and the others too." [92]

So here you have a woman who exemplifies leading like a woman using her power *to*, not power over. I asked her when she realized this about herself and Rupa replied, "The day I landed in this country as an immigrant was a very revealing experience, as most certainly, you look at your identity just as a number. But the hard question to ask yourself is, Does my number have any context in this newfound world? Do I belong? And what [is] it to find your sanctuary? To reimagine your existence? I did! Within days in this country, I cold-called every single company [where] I thought I could have value. Within a few days, I got an appointment with one of the top Hollywood agents, and I didn't leave the conversation until I got the job. I was almost seven months pregnant when I first got the job and only one month in the United States. I realized that I had the power to present myself to the world. I have the power to shine in my brilliance. I have the power to redefine every rule. If I can do it, you can do it."

Even through the pandemic, Rupa was more unreasonable than ever. Witnessing unprecedented challenges in business over the course of a few months, and without predictions of what the future might hold for her own business, her organization expanded its digital capacity to be even more resilient to future challenges. One such initiative was to develop learning communities with only a one- or two-click experience across every device from mobile phones, to tablets, as well as desktop computers. The integration of human-centered design thinking to help migrate virtual teams' workloads so collaboration is both measurable and scalable was a top priority for Rupa's organization to thrive during a pandemic.

Her advice to other women leaders is, "As humankind is under siege, everything we know is invalid, and it is time to unlearn and embrace new kinds of thinking. We are not entering to [a] new future, but we are *creating* a new one; women are architects of the new world order."

That's fabulously unreasonable, possibly the biggest moon shot ever attempted. I'm all in and I'm hoping, or rather intentioning, that you are too.

Leadership Intentioning Tool #8: Turn Implicit Bias on Its Head . . . because you can make its effects your superpowers.

> *For there is always light,*
> *if only we're brave enough to see it*
> *If only we're brave enough to be it.*
> —AMANDA GORMAN

The 22-year-old first national youth poet laureate of the United States stood at the podium where Joe Biden and Kamala Harris had just been sworn in as the U.S. president and vice president. Looking radiant in her sunshine yellow coat, braided hair held high by a wide crimson band, Amanda Gorman mesmerized America as she recited her poem, "The Hill We Climb."

From growing up with thickly accented immigrant grandparents, I have an ear for speech patterns. So I caught the occasional missing "r." I thought at first it was simply immature voice or an accent I couldn't recognize. Then I learned that Gorman (not unlike Joe Biden and a previous poet laureate Maya Angelou) had been challenged as a child with a speech impediment that she struggled to overcome. And we all know that anyone with what society deems a disability is often subjected to biases against them. Speech impediments are so tangible that children with them are quite likely to be judged less intelligent than their peers.

Now speaking in front of the entire nation—indeed the world—sharing the stage with the likes of JLo and Lady Gaga, and with the president and members of Congress looking on from behind the podium where she spoke, she showed no sign of insecurity. In fact, it turns out she regards the obstacle she had to overcome as a boost to her literary superpowers. She told the *Los Angeles Times*,[93] "I don't look at my disability as a weakness. It's made me the performer that I am and the storyteller that I strive to be. When you have to teach yourself how to say sounds, when you have to be highly concerned about pronunciation, it gives you a certain awareness of sonics, of the auditory experience."

Amanda Gorman had intentioned her way to that podium—and has already declared her intention to run for president in 2036 when she'll be old enough. This same intentioning process can turn culturally learned characteristics that put women on the receiving end of judgments rooted in implicit bias (otherwise known as racism, sexism, homophobia, anti-Semitism, and so forth) into our superpowers.

It's not only that "whatever doesn't kill you makes you stronger," as the saying goes, there is actually a learning process, a neurological rewiring in a sense that trains us to cope. For some, like software engineer Sailor Ghoul, whose abusive job experience led her to take a short-term disability leave and to be diagnosed with PTSD, some kinds of stress can become too much to bear. Yet in that coping, we can turn bias on its head, reframe it, tame it, and take advantage of the new behavior patterns it teaches us that propel us to success, as it did for Sailor when she left that company and created her popular software developer and tech podcast *Git Cute*.

And that is why companies with more women in their leadership make more money, why adding women to a previously all-male group raises group intelligence, and why countries led by women have managed the coronavirus more effectively. Because the culturally learned socialization that has created an intention gap for women has also created coping mechanisms, skills, and behaviors that are exactly what the world needs most now.

So I invite you to turn every implicit bias to which you have been subjected on its head and make its effects your superpowers. It's the leading edge of change leadership. In turning the implicit bias you have experienced into your superpowers, whether you are a woman, a person of color, an LGBTQ person, or anyone else others have tried to put in a box, you can instill best practices for inclusion to boost intentioning in the workplace and elsewhere.

But first, you must publicly unpack implicit bias of your own and others. Only then can you leach its negative effects out of your own head and reshape your brain to be more empathetic, collaborative, and emotionally intelligent. Turning implicit bias on its head can help create a culture where all can thrive.

Paradoxically, we can leap from ambition to intention by embracing the very parts of ourselves that have been devalued, categorized as "female" and therefore, of lesser value. These are behaviors we're told are wrong with us even though they're exactly what's right with us!

I say that millennia of oppression give us the advantage of a deep desire to change the narrative and transform the power paradigm. Our socialization has provided women the very attributes that make us so effective today: creativity, intuition, empathy, vulnerability, diplomacy, self-awareness, connection, nurturing, multitasking, and authenticity.

Heli Rodriguez Prilliman realized this when she said, "Whatever you think is a weakness of yours can be turned into a strength. Maybe you didn't go to Harvard. Maybe you're a single mom or an undocumented immigrant, or LGBTQ and your family have rejected you. All those experiences can be turned into a strength and you can use those stories to propel you forward. Think to yourself, 'I can get there because it made me strong, made me resilient, made me empathetic.' Think, *'It made me able to juggle 500 things at once.'*"

Minda Harts explores "white workplace behavior" extensively as it relates to white male leaders. I believe that intentioning comes easier to those with privilege and at the present time white men, especially tall ones, stand at the top of the privilege tree. So it is imperative that women exercise intentioning skills if we are ever to reach leadership, power, and pay parity.

The same applies beyond the corporation and into entrepreneurship. Female-led startups were getting just 3.4 percent of traditional investment capital before the pandemic; now that has declined to 2.3 percent.[94] This could be attributable once again to women leaving the workforce and putting their own intentions on hold for caregiving purposes during the pandemic, but it could also reflect a pandemic-induced implicit bias against female founders on the part of investors. Whatever the cause, the number is pathetic. And it is self-defeating because women-led startups are more likely to succeed and therefore are smarter investments.[95]

Nathalie Molina Nino is an investor, entrepreneur, and all-round visionary who has written a guidebook for women entrepreneurs to succeed in funding and growing their businesses in this implicit-bias driven world of investment capital. The book, *Leapfrog: The New Revolution for Women Entrepreneurs,* contains dozens of hacks to help women get their businesses funded; many of them, such as how to cash in on the woman (or minority) card, are exactly in this wheelhouse of turning implicit bias into your superpower. The obstacle is the path as the Zen saying goes.

Both Minda and Nathalie speak intentionally to an intersectional audience. We've discussed that intersectionality is a theoretical framework for understanding how aspects of a person's social and political identities might combine to create unique modes of discrimination and privilege. Intersectionality identifies advantages and disadvantages that are felt by people due to a combination of factors. Implicit bias is baked into centuries of discrimination and privilege largely related to gender, race, and class. Unraveling it is difficult since our minds are designed to organize by category.

When I teach my Women, Power, and Leadership class at Arizona State University, I always have about 25 percent men in my classes, and they get just as much out of my teachings about women and power and leadership as the female students do. Some of them are nervous at first and have a small chip on their shoulder because the course has the word "women" in the title. But they quickly become fascinated by the statistics about gender disparities as they relate them to their mothers, wives, sisters, and female partners. Because, you see, as soon as it becomes personal, they realize they don't want their female colleagues to bear the brunt of the negative aspects of implicit or systemic bias. And that is how we engage men as partners in overcoming biases rather than reinforcers of biases in the workplace, home, and culture.

The course is received a little otherwise by my female students. By the time they are juniors and seniors, most of them are working in some capacity and they're beginning to get a glimmer that, although they're told they can do anything they want, the men around them are getting treated differently, often in subtle ways that they are struggling to understand. Also, because each year the new wave of college students is increasingly diverse, there are always women coming in from cultures where they have fewer rights. They are ambitious and intentional about what they want to achieve, but their families may be entrenched in environments that, like the one I grew up in, are male dominated and don't encourage women to have careers. So these young women are often struggling with how to pursue their own dreams without losing their families, just as I struggled with that same tension. This has been particularly true for Latinas and Muslim women in my classes. They need to see representation to overcome limiting beliefs. They need encouragement to uncover themselves and allow their brilliance to shine.

I was thrilled to celebrate the watershed year of 2018 for women in U.S. politics, a decade after I was incensed enough about the lack of women in elected offices to write *No Excuses*. I felt a whole new arena of intentioning opening up!

As reported by the Center for American Progress, the 2018 elections brought a surge of new women to local and statewide offices, with notable gains for young women and veterans; historic wins in Senate and governors' races; and major breakthroughs for women of color in the House of Representatives.[96] Then, in 2020, the numbers climbed even further, to 27 percent of Congress.[97] Women now hold 30.9 percent of state legislative seats, a number that has quintupled since 1971.[98]

And regardless of your political persuasion, you'll agree that the historic picture of two women—the most powerful American elected officials other than President Joe Biden—sitting behind the president as he delivered his first State of the Union speech on April 28, 2021, represents dramatic progress toward gender parity.

Given the current attention to police brutality rooted in systemic implicit bias against Black men and women, it's interesting to note that one widespread implicit bias training program was conducted for police officers across dozens of precincts in California, spearheaded by the then-state's attorney general and now Madame Vice President Kamala Harris. That training was implemented in 2015.[99] But the term "implicit bias" was first coined in 1995 by psychologists Mahzarin Banaji and Anthony Greenwald. They opined that our behavior toward others is heavily influenced by associations and judgments that are unconscious or implicit.[100] We all have it to some degree or another if only because our minds need to organize our thoughts into categories in order to process the vast amounts of information we receive. But when this organization of information becomes a screen that puts other people into negative categories, its purpose is not so benign.

Intentional diversity in leadership and representation of women and other underrepresented groups across every sphere organically decreases those implicit biases that hold leaders and workers alike back from an infinite pie, power *to* way of thinking. In fact, recent research published in *Harvard Business Review*[101] found that firms with more women in the C-suite literally think differently, in several important ways. First, they are 10 percent more open to change while at the same time they become 14 percent less overtly risk-seeking. Second, they shift their focus from mergers and acquisitions (which the researchers call "knowledge buying") to research and development (dubbed "building," and a more collaborative approach).

Finally, as many other studies have found, having more than one woman on the top management team, or at least one in any new smaller cohort of managers, are variables that further advantage companies.

So I am not encouraging more biases, but I am saying that where they exist we can intentionally turn them (as did the women in the C-suite in the previous study whether deliberately or not) into assets and even superpowers.

EXERCISE

List the ways in which you have privilege and the ways you do not have privilege. What are you doing to use your privilege to advance yourself and other women and underrepresented groups? How can you take what you've learned from the ways you do not have privilege and turn them into assets for yourself and others? What opportunities have the current disruptions and dual pandemics opened for you as a woman, a person of color, or someone who might have otherwise been disadvantaged in some way? What are you doing to fully utilize those opportunities?

9 Power Demons
- Thinking your organization is a meritocracy
- Recruitment process bias
- Promotion bias
- Biased performance evaluations
- Groupthink
- Blind spots or denial of blind spots
- Viewing diversity and inclusion as optional or extra
- Overuse of the need to label, categorize, compartmentalize
- Prioritizing easy, quick solutions over bright new ideas

INTENTIONAL WOMAN

Katica Roy, Tech-Savvy Ambassador for Gender Equity, on Turning Implicit Bias on Its Head with Help from AI

Gender equity has entered the ethos. Every CEO knows that to keep the company profitable and to avoid shareholder revolts, it's important to recruit and retain women and people of color in top leadership.

Note that I had to rewrite that sentence to make it gender neutral and therefore equal. In my first draft, I referred to the CEO as "he." Implicit biases are so deeply rooted in culture that even people such as myself, alert to sexism and other biases, fall prey to them from time to time. Researchers have found that both men and women initially think "man" when they think "leader." Biases are called *implicit* or *unconscious* precisely because they are just that, and therefore are much more difficult to eradicate than more tangible characteristics.

No one knows this better than Katica Roy, who gets intentioning in a sweeping way both as a gender parity issue and in developing unbiased applications of artificial intelligence.

Katica is a gender economist and the CEO and founder of Denver-based Pipeline, an award-winning SaaS platform that leverages artificial intelligence to identify and drive economic gains through gender equity. Pipeline launched the *first* gender equity app on Salesforce's AppExchange.

Melding her personal background with her professional expertise, Katica founded Pipeline using data science and technology to change the way companies view gender equity. A former programmer, user-interface/user-experience designer, and data analytics expert, Katica harnesses her unique combination of skills at Pipeline to bridge the gender equity gap, providing businesses with a fresh perspective around gender bias in the workforce and the data and tactical roadmap to eliminate it.

An award-winning business leader with more than two decades of experience in technology, health care, and financial services, Katica has a rare combination of expertise in and passion for gender equity, people analytics, and sales operations.

"The future of revenue is about utilizing artificial intelligence to enable employers to make decisions to maximize the potential of their workforce. When 78% of CEOs say gender equity is one of their top 10 priorities while only 22% of employees say that gender diversity is regularly measured and shared, the leaky workforce pipeline is not being addressed and leaving financial returns on the table. So how do employers identify the cracks in the workforce pipeline and improve their financial performance?" she asks.

When I talked to Katica, one of the first things she told me is that she has been the sole breadwinner for a decade and that her husband is a stay-at-home dad. Bravo/brava to both of them! And her backstory, before heading up Pipeline, is a clear narrative of being incensed and taking that experience of an injustice to propel her superpower—creating AI methodology to remove implicit bias from internal promotions.

In March 2020, she wrote for NBC News,[102] "While I was on maternity leave with my daughter a few years ago, my boss was fired. Within two weeks of returning to work from maternity leave, I went from managing one team of employees to managing three. A great opportunity, but there was a catch. My male colleague who was one job level higher than me had taken on one additional team and, as I later found out, received additional compensation for doing so. I received nothing. I went to my new manager and HR to ask them how they wanted to close this pay gap. To my surprise, they said nothing. At this point I knew I needed to do research. What were my rights in this situation? I found the Lilly Ledbetter Fair Pay Act, which changed the statute of limitations for equal pay. I called HR and said, 'This is a Lilly Ledbetter Issue, every time you pay me, the statute of limitations starts over. What do you want to do about it?'"

Drum roll, please! They paid Katica back wages and increased her salary. At the same time, the experience of fighting for pay equity left her wondering why should her children have less economic opportunity simply because their mother is the bread-winner? This propelled her commitment to close the gender equity gap first by reframing it as an economic issue (which she correctly describes as a massive one) and second by using her skills to create a way for companies to solve the problem of inequity with the use of artificial intelligence data and algorithms that help remove implicit bias from processes and procedures.

Caveat—it has been shown that AI is often biased depending on who creates those algorithms. So again, we see that systems can't solve all problems, but Pipeline Equity's products are a good place to start.

In April 2020, at the height of the pandemic in every corner of the globe, Katica wrote a call to action in her extensive "Economy and Industry" piece for *The Mandarin*. [103] It should be reprinted in every media outlet on earth, in my opinion. And I'll start with the brilliant intro: "Our response to COVID-19 is fundamentally a question of who we are. When we say that ensuring the well-being of half the world's population matters, do we believe it? Or do we say it to be diplomatic? Most indicators would suggest it's the latter, as we've spent decades admiring the problem of gender inequity with little to show for our efforts. Not one country in the entire world can say it has achieved equality among the genders."

Thank you, Katica! And my favorite line is, "We are rapidly exhausting our list of excuses when it comes to achieving gender equity." Absolutely no excuses!

For turning implicit bias on its head, Katica advises, "We are wired to keep us safe, not happy. Work on mindset. Meditate and pray in the morning to make sure you're on the path. There is always something to be afraid of; you can manufacture fear. Always have the end goal in mind and be flexible in how you get there. Trust yourself. Planning is good but don't be so tied to a plan that you are not flexible. Trade security for being able to decide when and how to be flexible."

In other words, clarity about what you are intentioning is a superpower that you can unleash if you give yourself permission, and if you turn those injustices in your path into inspiration to create the change you want to see.

Leadership Intentioning Tool #9: Clang Your Symbols . . . because symbols create meaning, and when you create meaning, you bring others into the story; that's the most essential function of leadership.

> *"When you look at a field of dandelions, you can either*
> *see a hundred weeds, or a thousand wishes."*
> —UNKNOWN

Say it again: When you create meaning, you can bring others into the story and that's the most essential function of leadership.

Our minds add meaning to visual communication and associations through use of interpretation. We seek meaning in everything around us. Therefore, anything can become a symbol that quickly embeds in our mind's tools. Symbols can drive change and communicate vision more powerfully than dry facts.

A great symbol, meme, or metaphor—I'll be using those words interchangeably—allows leaders to coalesce people around a vision, give them the courage, and move them to action: in other words, to build intentioning.

Metaphors literally help us think. They enable us to visualize and organize our thoughts so that we can go forward even, or perhaps especially, in tough times to achieve our mission. We can make the complex simple enough that our teams can unite and have the courage to do what seems impossible.

When Howard Schultz of Starbucks returned as CEO in 2008 to address a cascade of issues that threatened the organization's culture and future[104] he motivated employees to take on the difficult turnaround tasks, in part, with these words, "There's a metaphor Vincent Eades likes to use: 'If you examine a butterfly according to the laws of aerodynamics, it shouldn't be able to fly. But the butterfly doesn't know that, so it flies.'" In other words, he was saying to his team of employees at Starbucks, you can do the impossible too. The butterfly is a symbol of that.

Scott Jeffrey, founder of CEOsage,[105] a transformational leadership agency and resource for self-actualizing individuals, connects the relationship between symbols, archetypes, and emotions: "Archetypes are simultaneously images and emotions. An image becomes dynamic when charged with emotion. Without emotion, the image cannot speak to us. Symbolic images act as doorways to our inner world—the home of our fantasies, imagination, and emotions. Without emotions, life is, well, lifeless."[106]

Leaders benefit from using this Intentioning Tool "Clang Your Symbols" because symbols influence behavior. We are motivated by stories and images that ignite our feelings and emotions. Do you relate to any of the following? Do any of them in particular relate to you and your leadership style or gifts?

- Chess Metaphor: leadership as an expression of strategy.
- Telescope Metaphor: leadership as a means of building toward a vision.
- The Entrepreneur Archetype: leadership that starts with an idea, builds with a team, and actualizes a dream.
- Lightbulb Metaphor: leadership as an expression of creativity and the generation of new ideas.
- The Coach Archetype: leadership as a pathway to developing individuals.
- The Heart Symbol: leadership that acts and serves with humility and grace.

Humans love symbol-rich stories such as those found in the movie *Star Wars*; their characters become memes and their storylines become metaphors that, in turn, become organizing principles for ideas. How many girls have embraced Wonder Woman for the strength and integrity she represents? Excuse me while I practice getting answers with my lasso of truth.[107]

I was impressed by the way Meghan Markle touched the world through the power of the symbols she chose for her wedding to Prince Harry. Every minute act and every tangible article in any royal wedding is imbued with symbolic meaning whether intended or not. But there is no question that this bride and groom thought through each nuance in exquisite awareness that the unique characteristics of their marriage ceremony gave them a historic opportunity to make symbolic statements about gender, race, and justice, thereby changing how people globally would feel and think about these pivotal issues.

Let's start with the most enduring and, in my opinion, most important symbol: the titles they chose to denote their status hereafter as Duke and Duchess of Sussex. By taking their titles from an antislavery predecessor, Meghan and Harry staked out an ethic of social justice as their abiding value. That symbolic value guided the rest of their wedding choices, from music to their mothers' roles: Harry by leaving space literally for his late mother Princess Diana and Meghan by having her African-American mother taking space visibly, if not centrally, in the church.

More importantly, use of these symbols in ways that the most effective leaders utilize them signal how they intend to live and lead. The Sussexes signaled their values and intentions before they subsequently eschewed the trappings of royalty altogether. This break with tradition was further symbolized by moving to the United States, issuing a formal statement that they would no longer be working with the British royal family, and revealing personal traumas in media interviews. However, the couple's immediate high profile in the U.S. is itself symbolic of the public's fascination with royalty. And Meghan continues to signal subtly with her attire, such as her feminist proclivities, by wearing a necklace, perhaps with her daughter in mind, that combines the Venus symbol with a protesting fist when she spoke at a Global Citizens charity concert.[108]

Four Ways Leaders Can Use Symbols Effectively

1. Create a framework of shared meaning that enables people to coalesce around an idea or action.

The late Warren Bennis, himself an iconic symbol of leadership expertise, often said that the first responsibility of a leader is the creation of meaning. Hearing him say this when I was early in my CEO career was the most useful piece of advice I ever received.

Simply being in a leadership role sends symbolic messages. People change how they look at you. Every word, every act is imbued with meaning. If you are not aware and intentional about the symbolic meaning you want to communicate, you will be defined by other people's fantasies about you. In the absence of deliberate information, people fill in the blanks.

Brands, avatars, and team mascots are the most obvious symbols leaders use to keep people feeling connected and aligned. While Arizona State University's Sun Devil mascot has always been prominently featured at sports events, I have noticed that recently everyone employed by the school features "Go Devils" in their email signoffs, a deliberate strategy by leadership to create visible symbolic cohesion.

And speaking of sports symbols, the NFL incorporating "Lift Every Voice" is a stunning example of the importance of symbols.[109] The lesson is that change is possible even in one of the most hyper-masculine "power-*over*" cultures. And it may be a "business decision" to sing the traditional Black anthem, but who cares? It will change minds and hearts at the same time it acknowledges the centrality of Black players.

2. Enable people to grasp a new idea or adopt a possibly controversial course of action.

That Markle wore a veil at all, not to mention the white dress and tiara, was a symbol that she would respect tradition in a culture that values its history and has a strong sense of propriety. But it was the obvious and subtle departures from tradition that most defined the meaning of this royal wedding and demonstrated how an entire culture can be led toward change by connecting the old symbols with the new ones you want to prevail.

Markle's very being as a biracial woman signals a dramatic shift in the notions of who owns power and privilege in Western society that has been held in white male hegemony for so long. Seeing a biracial woman in the role of British royalty, the ultimate symbol of white privilege, makes all of us who have been outsiders to the predominant culture smile. But for Black girls and women, it's a total game-changer in how they can see themselves in the story of social acceptance and leadership opportunities. Markle and Harry articulated with symbols many positive values: having Bishop Michael Curry deliver his sermon about love in Black church tones rather than the British accent usually heard in St. George's Chapel, and the Kingdom Choir singing "Stand By Me"—it can't get more symbolic than that—was my favorite part.

3. Call people to higher (or lower) values.
Symbols can unify. Once I was engaged in a heated conversation about what course of action a coalition group of peers should take in a challenging situation. There were multiple opinions and since no one was in charge of anyone else, there was no leader with the legitimate authority to call the discussion quits and choose a direction. Then one woman pulled out a bag of marbles and asked each of us to take one. "This is your touchstone," she said, referring to our shared mission. Such a simple action enabled the group to test courses of action back to the values we felt most passionate about and to let go of ego and individual agendas. The group quickly came to a decision and the conversation could proceed to the assignment of responsibilities for getting to the ultimate goal we all wanted to accomplish.

But like power, symbols can divide as well as bring people together. Religious symbols, for example, carry immense power to call people to their higher selves or lead them to the arrogant belief that they have the right to assume they have the only truth. And quasi-religious symbols, such as Ku Klux Klan hoods, can equally call people to their most base values and objectives. The results are all in the intention of the leader and the choice of symbols.

4.Shape cultures.

If one is cynical, we can predict that we will surely see more soaps and cosmetics take on girl power themes because feminism sells now. But cultures are complex, and each symbol tells a story or part of one. Humans learn through stories, and these narratives help us make sense of the world. For a leader, symbols are shorthand messages that allow followers to see themselves in the stories she tells about her vision or he tells about the new initiative for which he's soliciting support. And sometimes symbols are simply used to help people collaborate on their work despite different interests and opinions about the best way to reach a goal.

EXERCISE

What emojis do you use to symbolize love or laughter or affirmation? Are you drawn to red or blue based on your political proclivity? Are you wearing a heart or cross pendant? Lion or phoenix? Triangle or circles? Do you have favorite brand logos? Nike's swoosh perhaps because it has come to symbolize the company's strong stance on racial justice? Apple's apple with a bite out of it that signals design quality with a sense of humor? Maybe you start smelling the coffee when you see the Starbucks' siren logo? Look around you and take note. Then consider this: what is the symbol of *you*? What is your story, your singular message to the world, the visual representation that you want to show as a symbol of your core values and the intentioning you are building with your vision, courage, and action?

9 Power Demons

- Neglecting to continuously learn, study, and read
- Being absent from important group conversations or designating others to oversee them
- Mechanically fixating on productivity rather than fusing emotion and creativity
- Lacking knowledge about other cultures
- Disconnection to feelings
- Dismissing romance, fantasy, and daydreaming as fruitless

- Failing to tap into imagination or thinking it is all child's play
- Writer's block
- Intentioning without strategy

INTENTIONAL WOMAN

Elma S. Beganovich, Influencer—the Current Symbol of Authority

As a superstar marketer and social media influencer, Elma Beganovich's goal is to make brands explode digitally by helping them identify epicenters of influence, develop original and memorable campaigns, reach target audiences, and bring the brand storytelling into the future. And brands are above all, symbols. Companies spend millions of dollars and a great deal of time choosing their brand stories, promises, and looks.

The company, Amra & Elma, A&E, is both a symbol unto itself and a creator of symbols for its clients.[110] Elma founded A&E with her sister, Amra, and together, they claim a massive piece of cyberspace with over 2 million followers across social channels. The company is consistently named as top digital marketing experts, having operated the whole social show for 150+ big brands such as Nestle, LVMH, Uber, and Johnson & Johnson. Their intentioning purpose revolves around symbols that sell, content that shines, and all-in-one campaigns.

Now, even though I am a self-proclaimed junkie for social media posting and scrolling, what I'm most impressed by is Elma's life story leading to her know-how in storytelling and branding. Early hint: She's also an attorney.

Elma's family moved from Sarajevo, Bosnia, to the United States when she was 10 years old, which she thinks may have made her a little more resilient and tougher, edging into an entirely new culture so young in her life. Her parents, a doctor and structural engineer, left because of the war in much the same way that Marina Arsenijevic made the decision to come to America. And not unlike Marina, Elma seems naturally designed for the American dream. She studied government and French at Georgetown before pursuing law at University of Miami Law School, and (breath) then returning to Georgetown for specialization in financial regulation. A multifaceted intentioner!

Enter social media. No, really. When Facebook acquired Instagram in 2012, Elma and Amra were among the first to build a following by word of mouth through friends. There were only a handful of influencers at the time, but the platform was so receptive to visuals, which was perfect for what A&E did best—show off brands not by advertising them but by wearing them. Elma could see the potential that other people didn't see yet. She also credits her creative sister for this vision and foresight. The idea of spreading ideas virally and organically soon became a "thing" that everyone aspired to do, but Amra and Elma were already way ahead of the curve.

They seized upon an opportunity to provide women with totally attainable and relatable fashion, cosmetics, styling, and travel content, which set the stage for their blog. Three months into their endeavor, they had amassed 100,000 views. Because of this audience, which was considered huge at the time, Elma opened a Twitter account to reach outside of her circle of friends and family, focusing again on lifestyle and travel. The immediate interest excited her enough to leave the practice of law.

Opportunity continues to grow for this entirely digital company. Diverse populations are drawn to different visuals and symbols online, and this pair of sisters is dominating the infinite digital pie (or "slaying it," as they say). Between them, they have 2 million followers on social media.

Even at a time when budgets may be on pause, Elma told me, a shift in mindset due to the pandemic is only strengthening the online economy. As such, brand partnership and social media campaigns will only get more tightly woven into most organizations' advertising and marketing budgets. And what do users and brands see? Symbols of what they want to purchase—symbols that stand for something, even more so since social responsibility is top of mind for so many consumers now. Consider the bet Nike made by visibly supporting San Francisco 49ers quarterback Colin Kaepernick after he stirred controversy by "taking a knee" to call attention to police brutality and racism.

When looking at a prospective account, Elma asks, "What messages are they giving to clients?" She advises her clients, "Do not go dark on social—your clients and customers will remember what you have done for your community during the pandemic. You must stay present. Donate food or masks. Do something to keep engaging with your consumers." All these are symbolic acts, but they pack *real* meaning.

As this 35-year-old was dropping so much digital knowledge on me, I became increasingly curious about when she knew she could keep intentioning higher and higher. "When was the defining moment?" I asked. Her answer was a simple but symbolic one.

It was the moment that she and Amra went from making $99 per post to $20,000 per post! For women, Elma explains, financial ability is the symbol of power and self-sufficiency. Even through setbacks, including the time they invested in the wrong software and lost a lot of money as well as time, Amra and Elma knew that earning one's own money is essential, symbolically and tangibly, to enable you to move toward your full intention.

Even in the surreal times we are living in, A&E is well-positioned to pivot. Elma aspires to earn the same number of contracts as any big agency, which means she won't be humble about it. Her advice to other women about their careers is: "Don't take setbacks personally and don't punish yourself. Learn the lessons from the experience and move on quickly. Don't be afraid to negotiate aggressively if you think what you have is excellent, because there is so much opportunity in the digital space. Don't wait. You can be all the things you want to be in life."

Yes, you can. And to that I'll simply add this reminder: A leader starts with the symbolic power of the position. Everyone is watching you and reading meaning into your every move. Therefore, what you do with that positional power is up to you. It's all about how you create meaning for others through the use of the particular symbols with which you choose to identify yourself and your own leadership. Clang your symbols carefully and with robust use of your three powers of intention—Vision, Courage, and Action—to propel you to your boldest and most successful intentioning.

PART III

INTENTIONING GENDER PARITY IS A MOVEMENT…AND IT INCLUDES MEN

CHAPTER 9

••••••••••••••••••

AND WHAT ABOUT THE MEN?

I'm often asked, "What about the men? Aren't you leaving them out of the picture?" Or I'll hear, "I know lots of men who are very pro women." Alternate versions include: "I hired the first woman VP" or "I have two daughters," and so forth. These are the gender versions of "Some of my best friends are____." (You fill in the blank.)

Jimmie Briggs, founder of Man Up, journalist, and principal at the Skoll Foundation, really told it like it is when he said, "True racial equity is impossible without gender equality and safety."[III]

I 100 percent agree that we will only reach full equality and parity when men and women are working together for it. My husband, Alex Barbanell, has always been supportive of women's rights. He has marched and lobbied and advocated for women as long as I have known him. I am deliberately naming him because he proudly identifies as a feminist and has the t-shirts to prove it. Also, because he likes to be credited—he does have that much of a male ego. He even won the Martin Abzug Supportive Spouse award from the National Women's Political Caucus, an award named for the husband of the late Bella Abzug, the trailblazing congresswoman from New York.

And there are so many men I will shout out who are highly intentional partners (I do not like the term "ally" because it conveys the very power imbalance I aim to eliminate). I'll start with my father, Max Feldt, who from my birth always told me I could do anything my "pretty little head desires." I had to become an adult before I fully appreciated that message, but I am sure it had a lot to do with the growth of my intentioning over time.

I am grateful to men such as David Smith and Brad Johnson whose books and corporate programs show men why they should mentor women and how to do so productively—more on that follows. I so appreciate men such as Josh Levs, who was willing to stand up for fathers' rights to have parental leave, suing CNN in order to be able to care for his children and his wife who had experienced health issues after the birth of their third child. Then there are politicians including U.S. Senator Benjamin Cardin (D-MD), lead sponsor of Senate Joint Resolution 1, proposing that Congress extend the deadline for ERA (Equal Rights Amendment) ratification.

I applaud men such as Jimmie Briggs for his clarity of vision about the connection between racial and gender equality and for having done so much to eradicate sexual violence. Cheers for men such as award-winning composer, lyricist, actor, and creator of the musicals *Hamilton* and *In the Heights*, Lin Manuel Miranda, who has never hesitated to use his incredible talents and celebrity to support women's causes such as the UN's HeForShe initiative[112] and the 2017 Women's March. At the risk of leaving deserving men out of this list, I'll also name my friend Vada Manager, who stands up for women in his professional life by promoting projects like the film *On the Record* exposing sexual assault and harassment in the music industry, and Leon Silver, who has given decades of leadership for reproductive rights and currently is a Take The Lead board member. Last, I have been blessed with incredible male mentors throughout my career, in addition to female mentors, without whose essential guidance and sponsorship I might not be in conversation with you today.

But here's the thing:

••

We are in the midst of an unfinished revolution when it comes to gender equality.

••

This isn't my opinion; read the data and do the math.

No question, regardless of how far we have come, full gender equality won't be achieved without the partnership between women and men who share the vision of a universe where each of us can give our particular gifts to the world, and where each of us is free to embrace our power to go about intentioning the lives and careers of our choice.

At this stage of social change, it becomes more complicated to get to the finish line of gender parity in leadership by 2025. Here are three reasons why: differing generational perceptions, simple power dynamics even among well-meaning men, and the inevitable push back. Of course, I will share what to do about each of these.

Next Gen and Gender

When you have seen female firsts in almost every role, it becomes harder to realize that any gender differences in opportunity exist. Younger women, like Amanda Nachman, who is the CEO and publisher of *College Magazine*, which reaches 9 million students online at 200 college campuses nationwide, see far fewer gendered discrepancies than older women. That is a good thing because we want girls and young women to grow up thinking that the world is their oyster. We have worked hard to give them the belief that they can do or be whatever they intention themselves to do or be.

But those factors keep them from realizing that work remains to be done for women to have a level playing field and equal opportunities for top leadership roles.

Amanda is also the author of *#Qualified: You Are More Impressive Than You Realize,* published in August 2020, and it was in that context that I had the opportunity to interview her. The book is a guide on how to be successful in college and beyond.

Amanda told me that she hasn't seen gendered differences in the needs of the students she reaches. Instead she sees males and females having all the same concerns she coaches them to overcome in her book.

As we talked, Amanda thought further about the subject and observed, "Most likely women feel it more. Right now the gender inequality is not as visible, but we do see who is at the top and the pay disparity." She also said she noticed men have more confidence than women.

Perhaps I had put the idea into her head, and it is certainly possible for people to carry two competing ideas in their minds at the same time. For Amanda has also started a project to get to a 50/50 balance of women and men in political office. She is an intentional woman to be sure, in that she said she never once felt like she had to make her projects smaller. She has an ambitious plan to monetize her book with courses and other products as well. I'm in awe of her, and at the same time know that we cannot overlook the remaining journey ahead to achieve equal pay, power, and positions, and that it's essential for young women like herself and for men as well to be engaged in the change if we are to reach the finish line.

Power Dynamics

••

Despite facts, men in power are resistant to relinquishing theirs,

absent a transformation in how they are thinking about power.

••

The business case for women's leadership has been known for decades now. Greater gender parity increases profits by approximately 15 percent, improves company culture, and fosters innovation. Companies that fail to include women as equal partners in leadership leave half of the most educated talent on the table, given that women earn almost 60 percent of college degrees. Most people agree gender equality is the right thing to do.

But fairness alone rarely wins the day. We have reached a strategic inflection point where the business case and the fairness case have merged, and there are increasing pressures on leadership to take action on their diversity and inclusion goals, including gender parity. It's a moment any smart business should want to make the best of. So why are women still so far from parity?

Let's face it, no one relinquishes power easily, and usually not voluntarily if they are thinking in traditional power narratives. What Laura Liswood, Secretary General of the Council of Women World Leaders, called a "thick layer of men," specifically white men, still exists at the top of most major companies, governments, and even large nonprofits. It's not, repeat distinctively *not*, because women bail out at midcareer due to lack of ambition. It's not, repeat distinctively *not*, because women are twisted into knots trying to "have it all." It's not, repeat distinctively *not*, that having children causes women's careers to be truncated. It's that the men in power have not sufficiently moved over, sponsored women into higher positions, or created the flexible structures that all families need (and younger generations demand) today.

That's exactly why I teach and coach women to elevate their own intentioning in order to claim the positions where they can be the change they want to see. Women, after all, have the most immediate stake in change. And every other group mobilizes to advocate for itself—why shouldn't we?

But to make change at scale, we must make that essential shift from ambition to intention. And if it takes starting companies, structuring the cultures and policies as we want them, and growing these companies to sizes where we create bigger pies in the form of a more welcoming culture for gender parity, then so be it. That calls for substantial intentioning that women realistically still have to do.

Fortunately, there are women intentioning the way forward, such as Whitney Wolfe Herd, who in February 2021 became the youngest self-made female billionaire when she took her company Bumble public.[113] Bumble is a dating app where women must make the first move—talk about disrupting an entire culture! And the best part of Whitney's rise is that, echoing Kamala Harris's philosophy that she is the first female vice president but not the last, Herd said she doesn't intend to be the last woman to build a company of that magnitude. She recognizes her responsibility to other women to bring them along.

But back to the men. Overcoming resistance to feeling like they are relinquishing power is the most salient reason why the power transformation I propose from power *over* to power *to* is so important. It opens minds to realize there is an infinite pie of power. That's why making this conceptual shift is such a world-changer; it works for everyone's good and for all genders and diversities alike. Executive committees and boards can be enlarged to let in the fresh air of ideas from greater diversity. Founders can "pass the mic" as I am practicing often now to put women of color front and center instead of myself in Take The Lead's work. Organizations can create cultures of inclusion that span from intentionally valuing differences to making structural changes that allow both men and women to attend to family responsibilities while fulfilling their professional obligations to achieve their highest and best intentions. Male leaders can publicly champion laws and policies that make family leave and flexible working arrangements standard procedure. They can advocate for childcare as a social good and a necessary infrastructure investment.

The Push Back

....

I wrote a book for women called *No Excuses*. There are also "No Excuses"

for men, and many ways men can support gender equality.

....

If you've been in the world of women's rights for more than a minute, you know that for every step forward women make in the workplace or society, there will be an attempt to push us back to the previous, more comfortable (for men) state.

And just as surely, women will be blamed for causing the discomfort that social disruptions inevitably trigger. Yes, this still happens. When I spoke to an MBA class recently, a young male student asked, "What about women when they decide to take a long, paid vacation?" I asked what he was referring to. He said, "You know, maternity leave."

It wasn't long after women began declaring that they weren't going to tolerate sexual harassment in the workplace that articles began to appear in which men are portrayed as the victims of the sea change being wrought by women who seek merely to be allowed to pursue their professional ambitions and earn a living on an equal playing field. Men thinking that they are now somehow justified in refusing to meet with or mentor women in the workplace because there has been mounting pressure on them to reevaluate and alter behavior that was accepted in the past simply won't wash.

The #MeToo movement was initiated by Tarana Burke in 2006 and exploded in late 2017 as women increasingly became emboldened to speak publicly about their experiences with sexual harassment and violence.[114]

I recently was asked to make a speech about "After #metoo." I asked the audience these questions:

1. Would the women who have never experienced sexual harassment or abuse stand up? Only one did.
2. Would the men who can say you have never engaged in any behavior that could be considered sexual harassment or more stand up? Only two or three did.

This was an honest group.

Here's the deal: When men assume a level of privilege that leads to misuse of power in the form of sexual harassment, the consequences for women are profound. Women stand back and self-limit. They devalue themselves because they have been devalued, reduced to pieces of meat or eye candy.

• •

Sexual objectification, harassment, and abuse are about power, not about sex.

• •

If others can objectify you, this gets into your head; it causes you to be risk averse, not to hold up your hand or raise your authentic voice. Your humanity is eviscerated. You will never achieve equality because you have the enemy living in your thoughts telling you that you are unworthy. Your power goes from inside to outside of yourself. As a result, your intentionality often becomes lower than that of the man next to you because he knows he owns the world and you know only the world's limitations.

To overcome this pattern, it's essential that men and women work together as the equals they are in intelligence, skills, and capabilities.

An organizational consultant and a man I consider a mentor pointed out to me that even in non-workplace situations and without power imbalances, signaling sexual interest is complex and can be misunderstood by either party. Assigning blame, he notes, is not productive, but assuming best intentions can be.

I am convinced that most men and women today believe intellectually that defining and outlawing sexual assault and harassment, and giving credibility to women who allege them, are the right things to do. The stuck place is the challenging task of addressing the root causes in order to change behavior.

Companies are throwing millions at organizations that support women who have been abused in penance for their leaders' bad behavior. Yet as long as women are looked at as victims and women remain "in their place," little will change. Giving aid to a woman who has been abused is noble but creating a culture in which no woman or man is abused, and where women are afforded the respect of mentorship, is trans-formational. That transformation can only occur when men and women see themselves as equals in all aspects of life, and certainly in the workplace. *Flash*—it is possible to have dinner with someone without hopping into bed with her or him. A powerful man can mentor, advise, or sponsor a woman without harassing her. And if you do harass, it's not her fault.

Why Men Should Mentor Women: Help Comes from David Smith and Brad Johnson

Since men still hold the majority of powerful leadership posi-tions, it's incumbent on them to lead the way toward a more equal workplace. David G. Smith, PhD, professor of sociology in the Department of National Security Affairs at the United States Naval War College and the coauthor with Brad Johnson of *Athena Rising: How and Why Men Should Mentor Women*, explains why in an insightful *Harvard Business Review* article.[115]

Smith offers this tip for men who genuinely want to create more inclusive workplace cultures: "First, recognize that talented women mentees have to be challenged and receive critical feed-back and that this can be delivered in a way that demonstrates empathy, commitment, and unconditional regard. Second, being genuine and showing humility is often a gateway to developing a mentoring relationship without pretense. Finally, excellent mentors understand their mentees' strengths and weaknesses, and work to develop their mentees through providing opportunities and challenges that may be uncomfortable but enable a mentee to grow their confidence and skills as they progress toward their career goals and dreams."

How hard is that, gentlemen?

I tell women there are no excuses for them not to embrace their power and seek leadership roles. Indeed, this entire book is about intentioning. In that same light, there are no excuses for men not to mentor women so they can fully contribute the leadership potential organizations so desperately need. Here are some useful suggestions for them.

9 Tips and Tools for Men Who Are Partners for Gender Equality

1. Acknowledge your male privilege. Yes, regardless of culture, religion, or national origin, you have had it. But it's melting away fast, and you need to get ahead of the tidal wave. Gender is a cultural construct. At its core, it is a power construct. What are the messages you received growing up as a male in your culture? What messages did you receive about women? Write down all the stereotypes you heard about either gender and discuss them with a female friend or coworker. And be sure to create the future of your choice by raising boys differently.[116]

2. Change the power paradigm for yourself. Give up power *over*. Do not be complicit in it with other men. And shift to power *to*. This might take you on a personal hero's journey where you can discover the times you have been part of the problem, and where you can emerge at the other end as a better, stronger, and more effective leader and human being.

3. Yes, you can mentor women and even better, sponsor them. Here are a few tips: Have the meeting before the meeting with your mentee to make sure you will be able to support her ideas when she offers them. You'll be helping her overcome the most universally dismissive experience almost every woman has had. Recommend her for or assign her to stretch projects that will get her recognized as having high potential. Do that whether she is or isn't in the room.

4. Take this disruptive opportunity of the pandemic to #putwomenatthecenter of the recovery. That will help all families, possibly including your own, regain economic health, and enable organizations to retain or regain female talent.

5. In moments of culture-change opportunities like the one we are in, offer new ideas that propel yourself to the head of the pack as a leader for intersectional gender parity—be the role model/cultural broker/influencer/thought leader who helps to create a culture of inclusion.

6. Think about your daughter, your niece, your wife, your mother: What are your deepest convictions about how they should be treated? Now that the conversation has begun, take the #metoo moment to engage in conversation that redefines how to negotiate sexual tension. To do that successfully, you'll have to hear, listen, and seek to understand.

7. Be the (systems) change. You still own the keys to the kingdom, so you must be the ones who take the lead to unlock policy change at every level, personal, political, and organizational. Use your power to lead change for the greater good. And while you are at it, do your share of the wash and childcare.

8. Be a troll for good. Use the power of your voice to insist on equal voice for and respectful representation of women. Praise the stories fairly told and pan those that are sexist or noninclusive. Words matter. Images matter. Framing of the stories matter. Report trolls on social media and make positive statements that support gender and racial equality.

9. Share your journey. Be vulnerable enough to tell other men, and especially the boys in your life, how you embraced your power to change. The rewards will be incalculable.

CHAPTER TEN

WHAT YOU DO IS MORE THAN WHAT YOU DO

How We Reach Parity I Leadership by 2025

Things don't just happen; people make them happen in a systematic way. "Don't agonize, organize!" as labor movement leaders often say. It takes a movement, people working together to make systemic change. But someone has to start the ball rolling.

INTENTIONAL WOMAN

Former President and Chief People Officer of Salesforce Cindy Robbins Used Many Leadership Intentioning Tools—Such As Building Social Capital and the Infinite Pie—to Make System Change

A movement doesn't have to be big or loud. But it does have to have one clear characteristic: the intention that what you are doing is larger than yourself. Be aware that your every action impacts more people than those in your immediate circle. Sometimes, as with Cindy Guerra Robbins, it not only creates substantial change within a huge company, it creates change that extends outward, having an impact on many other companies that employ many thousands, if not millions, of people.

So remember that what you do is more than what you do. Your actions will always have a ripple effect of some kind, if for no other reason than we humans all live in a web of human connections. As you saw in Leadership Intentioning Tool #6: Build Social Capital, the world turns on human connections. Almost everything happens because of the people we know, associate with, work with, maintain close or loose relationships with. This is not a cold transactional fact; it is simply how most things happen. And Cindy is an A+ practitioner of building relationships. In fact, she attributes her ability to create and nurture relationships to her success in persuading the tech company Salesforce to eliminate its gender pay gap.

Cindy identifies as a "proud Mexican-American." She says she had two amazing parents who celebrated a 60-year marriage. She grew up in Del Rio, a small border town in Texas where her dad picked cotton and her mother was the major breadwinner who became a prominent real estate broker.

The family moved to Santa Clara, California, where Cindy was born. She went to Jesuit schools and became the first in her family to graduate from college. She credits her father with instilling a strong work ethic in her. He did jobs that were difficult but still left time for him to spend with the kids. From her mother, she learned valuable lessons about how relationships are an all-important aspect of how you go about your work. Her mother also taught her that she would encounter bias and that she would have to navigate it, but that it should never make her feel weak or different.

Cindy started working at Salesforce as a contractor, where she was impressed with the vibe and culture of the place and knew from the start that she wanted to be part of it. About six months later she became a team manager and worked her way up from there over a 14-year period to become the Chief People Person.

She credits her success with working hard but thinks it's her relationships that really helped, including those with mentors and sponsors. As her mentors were elevated, she was elevated too. One man in particular, George Hew, is still her mentor, and though he left Salesforce, he kept pressing her to achieve more and more, telling her she would eventually be the head of Human Resources.

George saw that the culture of a company changes with the company's growth, therefore it always needs new eyes and new people. He told Cindy she would have to take risks and grow, even though she didn't have the traditional background for the job. (Remember Leadership Intentioning Tool #4: Modulate Confidence.)

"I was happy," she told me. "My confidence grew. You get some wins along the way and you start to think about what is going to be most impactful." For example, Cindy saw that the maternity leave policy was, in her word, "awful," so she contributed to the culture changes that needed to occur in order to fix that. And she did!

Cindy was fortunate that her CEO, Marc Benioff, noticed there were few women at his quarterly meeting, and set a goal of having 30 percent women attend. Cindy and Leyla Seka, another Salesforce executive, were both invited to that meeting. People told them they needed to speak up more afterward. And the two women certainly took that advice!

Cindy and Leyla put their heads together and decided to hold a woman's summit. Cindy set up a meeting with Marc and though she realized it was a risk to bring up rumblings she had heard from employees about disparities in pay between men and women in comparable jobs, she proceeded to tell him that it would be better to lead on the issue because it would inevitably come up at the summit.

She already saw things shifting in the company—this was an important issue that was going to rise. It was the voice of the CEO who set the tone and could make equalizing pay happen.

"Pay is how people take care of their families and how you retain people for the long term—it's emotional," Cindy said. "I felt like we needed to lead. It's how we walk the walk. Women want to know they earned that seat at the table." Benioff agreed to support a compensation study of all 30,000 employees. To his surprise, even though he had set a value of equal opportunity, they found gender and racial related discrepancies among 6.6 percent of their employees. As a result, they made adjustments that first year (2016) totaling $3 million.[117]

They've continued these assessments and in subsequent years have made similarly sized adjustments. The reason that discrepancies continue, says Cindy, is that Salesforce has a practice of acquiring other companies whose pay scales then need to be brought into line with Salesforce's equal pay policies.

"Women have been dragging a gap for many years," she observed when we spoke. "And compensation is more than salary. So assessments will need to be conducted annually."

The company got an immense amount of positive media coverage as a result. Benioff clanged the symbols of CEO support for eliminating the gender pay gap frequently. The ripple impact of that leadership action caused other companies to follow suit.

But here's what's important about this story: Leyla and Cindy both realized they had greater responsibility, that they were in a position of power to influence the decision makers.

They realized that what they were doing was more important for the big picture and long haul than what they were doing to solve the immediate problem at Salesforce. They realized that their advocacy for equal pay would affect many thousands at Salesforce and many thousands, perhaps millions, as other companies took steps to eliminate their pay gaps. I mean, what company would want to be known as the one that has unequal pay?

Cindy said to me, "If you are in a position that has power, you have responsibility to do something." She attributes the success they had to having a partner in the endeavor like Leyla. "There is power in making change as a group—having that mutual support—two female executives from different divisions going together to the CEO was more powerful than if she had gone alone.

"We looked at each other and said, 'Well, this will either work out great or not.' We felt trust in one another and trust in doing it together. Women have to support each other."

You Are the Movement

I wanted to close this book with Cindy's story because I want you to leave this conversation realizing the enormous impact your own intentioning has on others as well as yourself.

Women often think that if they just work hard, somebody will tap them on the shoulder and offer them the next position. It doesn't happen that way. We must intentionally speak up for ourselves. When we do that, especially when joining with others, we can move the mountains that have blocked the path to parity for all women.

Powerhouse philanthropists MacKenzie Scott and Melinda French Gates joined together to create a movement for equality (see https://www.equalitycantwaitchallenge.org/), in the same way that Cindy Robbins and Leyla Seka joined together to get pay parity at Salesforce, and in the same way that any two women in a meeting may amplify each other's voices. No one has to do everything but everyone can do something to help move the dial to gender parity in leadership by 2025.

On the big systemic level, the same movement-building principles I shared previously apply to creating that culture of inclusion and reaching parity in leadership. It takes major intentioning. It takes being bold and carrying out, leaving the old adage to be calm and carry on in the dust. It takes vision, courage, and action. And it takes persistence.

Twenty years ago, would Tim Cook, CEO of Apple, have publicly said, "I am gay"? Maybe not. But now, not only can he do it, he is lauded for doing it. The "right" time didn't happen by itself. The time happened because people got together with intention and made it happen. That's a movement.

Studies have found that women value relationships that align with their higher purpose. Though that purpose may vary from woman to woman, most are looking to work with companies or organizations that express their own higher purpose or values in their actions. The most common reason women gave for staying with their current employer was that their job fits well with other areas of their life—followed by enjoying the work that they do and believing that their job gives them the opportunity to make a difference.

This is a perfect fit for intentioning the next step in advancing gender parity in all spheres of work and life, whether business, nonprofit/social profit, professions, government, philanthropy, or home.

••

The power paradigm shift, the "Lead Like a Woman" framework, and the "9 Leadership Intentioning Tools" in this book will prepare, develop, inspire, and propel you, women of all diversities and intersectionalities, *now* so that by 2025 women will have attained their fair and equal share of leadership positions across all sectors of industry and society.

••

What you do to achieve that goal will, without a doubt, be more than what you do.

Remember Melinda French Gates's wise words from her book *The Moment of Lift: How Empowering Women Changes the World*, "Because when you lift up women, you lift up humanity."

We simply cannot squander women's talents now, when so much hangs in the balance. By intentioning, you will be at the vanguard of reimagining and reconstructing a vibrant and sustainable future for us all. I look forward to intentioning right along with you.

••

For your own good and the good of others, and for good as in forever.

••

BE BOLD AND CARRY OUT: YOUR INTENTIONING ACTION PLAN AND MORE OPPORTUNITIES FOR ENGAGEMENT

Now that you know how to lead like a woman and you have your Leadership Intentioning Tools, your next step is to create your own Intentioning Action Plan so that you will get practice in using those tools. I have created a template to guide you anytime you are planning your next career move, need to solve a problem, or otherwise want to clarify your vision, courage, and action steps to achieve your intention. You will find the template at www. intentioningbook.com. It will always be there for you, so use it as many times as you like.

I invite you to continue the conversation at www.intentioningbook.com.

There you will find the downloads and exercises mentioned in this book, along with additional research, resources, book talks, and frequent fresh content.

I also invite you to join my private Intentioning community where you will meet other intentional women like yourself for mutual support, inspiration, and of course, *INTENTIONING*. Get details and sign up at www.intentioningbook.com. There you can also find how to bring me to speak at your book club, company, or convention.

Go to www.taketheleadwomen.com so that you will always be the first to know about our in-person and virtual training for women's leadership and DEI, coaching, and events for individuals and organizations. And be sure to sign up for our weekly newsletter to get the latest news about women and leadership.

Let's stay connected! I'm on all social media platforms (way too much) @GloriaFeldt.

Lastly but so very importantly, you can help all women learn the benefits of intentioning by spreading the word about this book and its messages. Tell your friends. Post reviews of *Intentioning* on Amazon, Indiebooks, Goodreads, and any of your favorite places to buy or talk about books.

Together, we can make sure that women of all diversities and intersectionalities reach parity in pay, power, and leadership positions by 2025!

••

Remember, what you do is more than what you do, and I thank you for all of it.

••

ACKNOWLEDGMENTS

It took more than a village to write this book, especially since I was also running a nonprofit organization during a global pandemic. I have so much gratitude for the many people who have made this book possible.

My first thanks go to the incredibly generous, passionate, intentional women I had the pleasure of interviewing when I first had the idea of building the Leadership Intentioning Tools around their stories. In many cases, they were kind enough to talk with me again when I realized I needed to find out if or how the pandemic changed their lives and careers.

Everybody thanks their editors but Hope Innelli gets an extra special level of appreciation not only for being a highly skilled editor who gets nuances and makes me so much better than I am, but also for leaping tall buildings in a single bound to meet impossible timelines with unfailing grace. In line with my belief that the world turns on human connections, thank you Cate Luzio for introducing me to Worth Media CEO Juliet Scott-Crawford, who connected me with Justin Batt, publisher of Worth Books, who in turn introduced me to Forefront Books publisher Jonathan Merkh, who quickly identified Hope as the right editing match. A virtuous circle if there ever was one to enable me to produce the book I want when I wanted, and in the way I *intentioned* to do it.

To the brilliant Jamia Wilson, the model of an intentioning female leader, you honor me deeply by writing the foreword. There is nothing more gratifying than for a younger woman who was once my mentee to leap far ahead of me and now show me what the future of leadership looks like.

Much gratitude to Anna Tropiano for research, helping me organize my disparate pieces of writing so I could turn them into a coherent whole, and for getting the endnotes done in record time.

Last but really first, I could never have written this book without my beloved husband, Alex Barbanell, feeding me, listening to me complain when I was frustrated or exhausted, giving up many evenings to my writing habit, and always, always being my biggest booster.

ENDNOTES

1   Courtney Connley, "Women's Labor Force Participation Rate Hit a 33-year
    Low in January, According to New Analysis," CNBC, February 8, 2021,
    https://www.cnbc.com/2021/02/08/womens-labor-force-participation-rate-
    hit-33-year-low-in-january-2021.html.
2   Ross Murray, "Millions of Women Lost Jobs in 2020 — Here's How They're
    Coming Back," Talent Blog, March 8, 2021, https://business.linkedin.com/
    talent-solutions/blog/trends-and-research/2020/many-women-rejoining-
    workforce-after-covid-cost-millions-job.
3   Deloitte Global, "Women @ Work: A global outlook," Deloitte, accessed
    May 19, 2021, https://www2.deloitte.com/global/en/pages/about-deloitte/
    articles/women-at-work-global-outlook.html?id=gx:2el:3pr:4women_at_
    work(womenatwork,_gender_survey):GC1000011:6abt:20210519.

Chapter 1

4   Amanda Taub, "Pandemic Will 'Take Our Women 10 Years Back' in the
    Workplace," *New York Times*, September 26, 2020, https://www.nytimes.
    com/2020/09/26/world/covid-women-childcare-equality.html.
5   Elise Gould, "The Economic Fallout of the Pandemic Has Had a Profound
    Effect on Women," interview by Lulu Garcia-Navarro, Weekend Edition,
    aired on January 31, 2021, on NPR.
6   Nicole Bateman and Martha Ross, "Why Has COVID-19 Been Especially
    Harmful for Working Women?," Brookings, October 2020, https://www.
    brookings.edu/essay/why-has-covid-19-been-especially-harmful-for-work-
    ing-women/.

Chapter 2

7   Gloria Feldt, "Where the Hell Are All the Women?—Hillary's Historic Run
    Left '18 Million Cracks in the Glass Ceiling,'" *Elle*, July 18, 2008, https://
    www.elle.com/culture/career-politics/a9270/where-the-hell-are-all-the-
    women-19704/.
8   Richard Fry, "U.S. Women near Milestone in the College-educated La-
    bor Force," Fact Tank, June 20, 2019, https://www.pewresearch.org/fact-

tank/2019/06/20/u-s-women-near-milestone-in-the-college-educated-labor-force/.

9   "No Excuses Media Buzz," Gloria Feldt, https://gloriafeldt.com/about-no-excuses/media-buzz/.

Chapter 3

10 Gené Teare, "Global VC Funding to Female Founders Dropped Dramatically This Year," Crunchbase News, December 21, 2020, https://news.crunchbase.com/news/global-vc-funding-to-female-founders/#:~:text=%E2%80%9COur%20portfolio%20is%20all%20about,to%202.8%20percent%20in%202019.

11 "The Cru Raises $2M!," video, Facebook, posted by Tiffany Dufu, October 21, 2020, https://fb.watch/5F5LxrtKFX/.

12 Ted Johnson, "Lawmakers Reach Deal on Covid-19 Relief That Includes $15 Billion for Movie Theaters, Live Venues," Deadline, December 20, 2020, https://deadline.com/2020/12/covid-19-relief-movie-theaters-live-entertainment-1234659887/.

Chapter 4

13 Kadeen Griffiths, "'Black Panther' Star Danai Gurira Didn't Let the World Tell Her What Black Women Could Be. She Showed Them.," Bustle, February 27, 2018, https://www.bustle.com/p/black-panther-star-danai-gurira-didnt-let-the-world-tell-her-what-black-women-could-be-she-showed-them-8250971.

14 "Danai Gurira Biography," IMDb, https://www.imdb.com/name/nm1775091/bio?ref_=nm_ov_bio_sm.

15 Julie Bosman, Kate Taylor, and Tim Arango, "A Common Trait among Mass Killers: Hatred toward Women," *New York Times*, August 10, 2019, https://www.nytimes.com/2019/08/10/us/mass-shootings-misogyny-dayton.html.

16 "You've Got to Be Carefully Taught," Wikipedia, https://en.m.wikipedia.org/wiki/You%27ve_Got_to_Be_Carefully_Taught.

17 "Equal Pay Day 2021," Equal Pay Today, http://www.equalpaytoday.org/equal-pay-day-2021

18 Tiffani Lennon, J.D., *Benchmarking Women's Leadership in the United States*, ed. Shelley Popke (University of Denver – Colorado Women's College, 2013), https://www.issuelab.org/resources/26706/26706.pdf.

19 Rosamond Hutt, "These 10 Countries Are Closest to Achieving Gender Equality," World Economic Forum, December 17, 2019, https://www.weforum.org/agenda/2019/12/gender-gap-equality-women-parity-countries/.

20 Kimberlé W. Crenshaw, *On Intersectionality: Essential Writings* (n.p.: The New

Press, 2017).

21   Campbell Robertson and Robert Gebeloff, "How Millions of Women Became the Most Essential Workers in America," *New York Times*, April 18, 2020, https://www.nytimes.com/2020/04/18/us/coronavirus-women-essential-workers.html?referringSource=articleShare.

22   Edward-Isaac Dovere, "Black Women Are Realizing the Power of Their Vote," *Politico Magazine*, February 13, 2018, https://www.politico.com/magazine/story/2018/02/13/atlanta-mayor-keisha-lance-bottoms-black-women-vote-political-power-216969.

23   "John Lewis Visits New Black Lives Matter Mural with DC Mayor," video, WHIO TV, June 8, 2020, https://www.whio.com/video/hot-video/john-lewis-visits-new-black-lives-matter-mural-with-mayor/lWoTBv2bJqUF7n-wIDnxuvO/.

24   Gillian Brockell, "At the 1963 March on Washington, Civil Rights Leaders Asked John Lewis to Tone His Speech down," *Washington Post*, July 18, 2020, https://www.washingtonpost.com/history/2020/07/18/john-lewis-was-last-living-speaker-march-washington-civil-rights-leaders-asked-him-tone-it-down/.

25   Jason DeParle, "What Makes an American?," *New York Times*, August 9, 2019, https://www.nytimes.com/2019/08/09/sunday-review/immigration-assimilation-texas.html.

26   Elizabeth Segran, "How Hiding Your True Self at Work Can Hurt Your Career," *Fast Company*, September 17, 2015, https://www.fastcompany.com/3051111/how-hiding-your-true-self-at-work-can-hurt-your-career.

Chapter 5

27   "The 1619 Project," *New York Times*, August 2019, https://www.nytimes.com/interactive/2019/08/14/magazine/1619-america-slavery.html.

28   Bas Hofstra et al., "The Diversity–Innovation Paradox in Science," *Proceedings of the National Academy of Sciences* 117, no. 17 (2020): 9284-91.

29   Anna Powers, "A Study Finds That Diverse Companies Produce 19% More Revenue," *Forbes*, June 27, 2018, https://www.forbes.com/sites/annapowers/2018/06/27/a-study-finds-that-diverse-companies-produce-19-more-revenue/?sh=3ccde2c5506f.

30   Matt Krentz, "Survey: What Diversity and Inclusion Policies Do Employees Actually Want?," *Harvard Business Review*, February 5, 2019, https://hbr.org/2019/02/survey-what-diversity-and-inclusion-policies-do-employees-actually-want.

31   Rebecca Greenfield, "The White-Male Mentorship Premium," Bloomberg, August 9, 2019, https://www.bloomberg.com/news/articles/2019-08-09/

white-male-mentorship-brings-a-premium-and-it-s-hurting-women.

32   Jeff Green, "Managers Pick Mini-Me Proteges of Same Race, Gender,"
     Bloomberg, January 8, 2019, https://www.bloomberg.com/news/arti-
     cles/2019-01-08/managers-pick-mini-me-proteges-of-same-gender-race-in-
     new-study.

33   Ben Hecht, "Moving beyond Diversity toward Racial Equity," *Harvard
     Business Review*, June 16, 2020, https://hbr.org/2020/06/moving-beyond-di-
     versity-toward-racial-equity.

34   Warren Buffett, "Warren Buffett Is Bullish … on Women," *Fortune*, May 2,
     2013, https://fortune.com/2013/05/02/warren-buffett-is-bullish-on-wom-
     en/.

35   Edward H. Chang et al., "Does Diversity Training Work the Way It's
     Supposed To?," *Harvard Business Review*, July 9, 2019, https://bg.hbr.
     org/2019/07/does-diversity-training-work-the-way-its-supposed-to.

36   "Report: The Bottom Line: Connecting Corporate Performance and Gender
     Diversity," Catalyst, January 15, 2004, https://www.catalyst.org/research/
     the-bottom-line-connecting-corporate-performance-and-gender-diversity/.

37   Sundiatu Dixon-Fyle et al., "Diversity Wins: How Inclusion Matters," McK-
     insey & Company, May 19, 2020, https://www.mckinsey.com/featured-in-
     sights/diversity-and-inclusion/diversity-wins-how-inclusion-matters.

38   "EY Report Highlights Benefits of Gender Diversity in Business," EY
     Financial Services, 2015, https://eyfinancialservicesthoughtgallery.ie/ey-re-
     port-highlights-financial-benefits-gender-diversity-business-internation-
     al-womens-day-2/.

39   Brenda Trenowden, "Gender Balance in Business," Bain & Company, March
     27, 2019, https://www.bain.com/insights/gender-balance-in-business-video/.

40   Bossoutrot Sylvie, Armine Grigoryan, and Amanda Green, "Gender Equal-
     ity: Why It Matters, Especially in a Time of Crisis," The World Bank, April
     13, 2020, https://www.worldbank.org/en/news/opinion/2020/04/13/gen-
     der-equality-why-it-matters-especially-in-a-time-of-crisis#:~:text=As%20
     the%20World%20Bank%20Group's,15%20percent%20of%20its%20GDP.

41   Belén Garijo, "How Gender Diversity at the Top Can Boost the Bot-
     tom Line - and Improve the World," World Economic Forum, April
     29, 2019, https://www.weforum.org/agenda/2019/04/gender-diversi-
     ty-makes-great-business-sense/.

42   Deloitte University, "The Radical Transformation of Diversity and Inclu-
     sion," Deloitte, 2015, https://www2.deloitte.com/content/dam/Deloitte/
     us/Documents/about-deloitte/us-the-radical-transformation-of-diversi-
     ty-and-inclusion-the-millennial-influence.pdf.

43   "Becoming Irresistible: A New Model for Employee Engagement," Deloitte,

January 27, 2015, https://www2.deloitte.com/us/en/insights/deloitte-review/issue-16/employee-engagement-strategies.htmlhttps://www2.deloitte.com/us/en/insights/deloitte-review/issue-16/employee-engagement-strategies.html.

44 Anu Madgavkar et al., "COVID-19 and Gender Equality: Countering the Regressive Effects," McKinsey & Company, July 15, 2020, https://www.mckinsey.com/featured-insights/future-of-work/covid-19-and-gender-equality-countering-the-regressive-effects.

45 Ashely Worley, "COVID-19 Is Reversing the Important Gains Made over the Last Decade for Women in the Workforce—PwC Women in Work Index," PWC, February 3, 2021, https://www.pwc.com/gx/en/news-room/press-releases/2021/women-in-work-index-2021.html.

46 Cordelia Fine, *Delusions of Gender: How Our Minds, Society, and Neurosexism Create Difference* (n.p.: W.W. Norton & Company, 2010).

47 Harvard, "Implicit Bias Test," Project Implicit, https://implicit.harvard.edu/implicit/selectatest.html.

Chapter 6

48 Leslie Albrecht, "Who Donates More Time and Money to Charity—Men or Women? Here's Your Answer," Market Watch, January 16, 2019, https://www.marketwatch.com/story/wealthy-women-give-away-their-money-and-time-more-than-rich-men-2018-10-24.

49 "Lynn J. Good," Duke Energy, January 8, 2021, https://www.duke-energy.com/our-company/about-us/leadership/lynn-j-good.

50 "#50WomenCan Change the World in Journalism," Take The Lead Women, 2020, https://www.taketheleadwomen.com/50womencan/journalism.

51 Gwen Moran, "7 Tricks for Making Good Decisions in Times of Crisis," Fast Company, April 29, 2020, https://www.fastcompany.com/90497257/7-tricks-for-making-good-decisions-in-times-of-crisis.

Chapter 7

52 "Breakthrough Diversity and Women's Leadership Solutions to Lead in the Workforce," Take The Lead Women, https://www.taketheleadwomen.com/.

53 "9 Leadership Power Tools to Advance Your Career," Take The Lead Women, https://courses.taketheleadwomen.com/onlinecourse.

54 Alice Hoekstra, "5 Questions to Help You Find Your Purpose," Thrive Global, July 13, 2018, https://thriveglobal.com/stories/what-is-a-purpose/.

55 Sande Friedman, "Girls Run the (Cheese!) World," Di Bruno Bros, March 5, 2019, https://blog.dibruno.com/2019/03/05/girls-run-the-cheese-world/.

56 The Harris Poll, Berlin Cameron, and The Female Quotient, *Female Lead-*

ership in the Era of #MeToo the Harris Poll Survey Results, December 2017, https://ml.globenewswire.com/Resource/Download/fec25583-ecb6-45f1-8b89-f9c40610065e.

Chapter 8

57   Maureen Dowd, "Lady of the Rings: Jacinda Rules," *New York Times,* September 8, 2018, https://www.nytimes.com/2018/09/08/opinion/sunday/jacinda-ardern-new-zealand-prime-minister.html.

58   Kenji Yoshino, " 'Covering' to Fit in and Get Ahead," News, August 26, 2015, https://www.hsph.harvard.edu/news/features/covering-to-fit-in-and-get-ahead/.

59   Victor Lipman, "Too Many Employees Feel the Need to 'Cover' Their Identities," *Psychology Today,* May 3, 2016, https://www.psychologytoday.com/us/blog/mind-the-manager/201605/too-many-employees-feel-the-need-cover-their-identities#:~:text=The%20authors%20discuss%20the%20notion,their%20identities%20in%20some%20way.%E2%80%9D.

60   The Lily News, "GoldieBlox Founder Debbie Sterling Is Transforming the Toy Aisle for Girls," The Lily, August 27, 2017, https://www.thelily.com/goldieblox-founder-debbie-sterling-is-transforming-the-toy-aisle-for-girls/.

61   Shellye Archambeau, https://shellyearchambeau.com/.

62   "#50WomenCan Change," Take The Lead Women.

63   Letter by Christina Tapper, "For Black Women Who Give Themselves License to Change the Rules," September 19, 2019, No. 12, Breaking Form.

64   Julia Pollak, "Studying More, Working More, Still Earning Less: Why the Gender Pay Gap Persists," ZipRecruiter Blog, December 3, 2018, https://www.ziprecruiter.com/blog/gender-pay-gap/.

65   Women's Campaign Fund, https://www.wcfonline.org/.

66   Skagen, https://www.skagen.com/en-us/.

67   Marina Arsenijević, http://www.arsmarina.com/.

68   Deborah Fuller, "3 Medical Innovations Fueled by COVID-19 That Will Outlast the Pandemic," The Conversation, March 9, 2021, https://theconversation.com/3-medical-innovations-fueled-by-covid-19-that-will-outlast-the-pandemic-156464.

69   Minda Harts, *The Memo: What Women of Color Need to Know to Secure a Seat at the Table* (n.p.: Seal Press, 2019).

70   "The Lift List," Lift Women Up, 2020, accessed May 25, 2021, https://www.drnancyoreilly.com/wp-content/uploads/2020/05/List.pdf.

71   Women Connect4Good, Lift Women Up, accessed May 25, 2021, https://www.drnancyoreilly.com/lwu/.

72   Julia Pimsleur, *Million Dollar Woman: The Essential Guide for Female Entre-*

preneurs Who Want to Go Big (Simon and Schuster, 2015).

73 Lacquerbar, 2019, accessed May 25, 2021, https://www.lacquerbar.com/.

74 Marissa Brassfield, "Study Shows Successful, Ambitious People Really Do Have It All," Payscale, March 15, 2012, https://www.payscale.com/career-news/2012/03/ambitious-people.

75 Watermark Conferences for Women, 2020, accessed May 25, 2021, https://www.watermarkwomensconference.org/about.

76 Gretchen Livingston and Kim Parker, "8 Facts About American Dads," Pew Research Center, June 12, 2019, https://www.pewresearch.org/fact-tank/2019/06/12/fathers-day-facts/.

77 "Soledad O'Brien," Wikipedia, accessed May 25, 2021, https://en.wikipedia.org/wiki/Soledad_O%27Brien.

78 "#50WomenCan Change," Take The Lead Women.

79 "About," Soledad O'Brien Productions, accessed May 25, 2021, https://soledadobrienproductions.com/about.

80 "Black in America," Wikipedia, accessed May 25, 2021, https://en.wikipedia.org/wiki/Black_in_America.

81 Tiffany Dufu, *Drop the Ball: Achieving More by Doing Less* (Macmillan, 2017).

82 Margaret Rhodes, "Tiffany Dufu," Fast Company, June 5, 2012, https://www.fastcompany.com/3010230/tiffany-dufu.

83 "Do What You Love: Thinking Big for Your Next Gig," video, Youtube, posted by Take The Lead Women, August 14, 2010, https://www.youtube.com/watch?v=Pyk4jFr1Ifs.

84 Mindy Wright, "CEO Spotlight: Nina Vaca, CEO at Pinnacle Group," CEO World Magazine, February 14, 2020, https://ceoworld.biz/2020/02/14/ceo-spotlight-nina-vaca-ceo-at-pinnacle-group/.

85 Celinne Da Costa, "How This Millennial Woman Built a 7-Figure Empire by Leveraging Human Connection," *Forbes*, January 30, 2019, https://www.forbes.com/sites/celinnedacosta/2019/01/30/how-this-millennial-woman-built-a-7-figure-empire-by-leveraging-human-connection/?sh=3e8465312c2c.

86 "Impacting Millions," Impacting Millions Enrollment, https://www.impactingmillions.com/.

87 Linda Stein, 2020, https://www.lindastein.com/home.

88 Bill Taylor, "The Best Leaders See Things That Others Don't. Art Can Help.," *Harvard Business Review*, April 18, 2018, https://hbr.org/2018/04/the-best-leaders-see-things-that-others-dont-art-can-help.

89 "#50WomenCan Change," Take The Lead Women.

90 Dinah Eng, "When Being Pushy Is the Key to Success," *Fortune*, December

27, 2019, https://fortune.com/2019/12/27/charlotte-jorst-success-ska-gen-kastel-denmark/.

91 "Who We Are," World Woman Foundation, accessed May 25, 2021, https://www.worldwomanfoundation.com/#:~:text=EQUALITY%20FOR%20WOMEN%20is%20progress,collaboratively%20for%20an%20equitable%20future.

92 John F. Kennedy, "Moon Speech," speech presented at Rice Stadium, September 12, 1962, NASA, https://er.jsc.nasa.gov/seh/ricetalk.htm.

93 Julia Barajas, "How a 22-year-old L.A. Native Became Biden's Inauguration Poet," *Los Angeles Times*, January 17, 2021, https://www.latimes.com/entertainment-arts/books/story/2021-01-17/amanda-gorman-biden-inauguration-poet?fbclid=IwAR2VVyw-Drxo3BRWnfVSZdCkPU_xipdQkxyN-fJkCHWrk1xNJ8TYfeqSkJoo.

94 Gené Teare, "Global VC Funding to Female Founders Dropped Dramatically This Year," Crunchbase News, December 21, 2020, https://news.crunchbase.com/news/global-vc-funding-to-female-founders/#:~:text=%E2%80%9COur%20portfolio%20is%20all%20about,to%202.8%20percent%20in%202019.

95 Allyson Kapin, "10 Stats That Build the Case for Investing in Women-Led Startups," *Forbes*, January 28, 2019, https://www.forbes.com/sites/allysonkapin/2019/01/28/10-stats-that-build-the-case-for-investing-in-women-led-startups/?sh=760bf87759d5.

96 Judith Warner, Nora Ellmann, and Diana Boesch, "The Women's Leadership Gap," Center for American Progress, November 20, 2018, https://www.americanprogress.org/issues/women/reports/2018/11/20/461273/womens-leadership-gap-2/.

97 Carrie Blazina and Drew Desilver, "A Record Number of Women Are Serving in the 117th Congress," Pew Research Center, January 15, 2021, https://www.pewresearch.org/fact-tank/2021/01/15/a-record-number-of-women-are-serving-in-the-117th-congress/.

98 "Women in State Legislatures 2021," Center for American Women and Politics, accessed May 25, 2021, https://cawp.rutgers.edu/women-state-legislature-2021.

99 State of California Department of Justice Office of the Attorney General, "Attorney General Kamala D. Harris Kicks off First-of-its-Kind Law Enforcement Training on Implicit Bias & Procedural Justice," news release, November 17, 2015, https://oag.ca.gov/news/press-releases/attorney-general-kamala-d-harris-kicks-first-its-kind-law-enforcement-training.

100 Mahzarin Banaji, "How the Concept of Implicit Bias Came into Being," interview by David Greene and Renee Montagne, *Morning Edition*, aired

October 17, 2016, on NPR.

101 Corinne Post, Boris Lokshin, and Christophe Boone, "Research: Adding Women to the C-Suite Changes How Companies Think," *Harvard Business Review*, April 6, 2021, https://hbr.org/2021/04/research-adding-women-to-the-c-suite-changes-how-companies-think?utm_medium=email&utm_source=newsletter_daily&utm_campaign=dailyalert_notactsubs&delivery-Name=DM126621.

102 Katica Roy, "Gender Economist Katica Roy: Want to Be a CEO? Don't Let This No. 1 Factor Hold You Back," NBC News, March 10, 2020, https://www.nbcnews.com/know-your-value/feature/gender-economist-katica-roy-want-be-ceo-don-t-let-ncna1154971.

103 Katica Roy, "Here's How to Achieve Gender Equality After the Pandemic," The Mandarin, April 27, 2020, https://www.themandarin.com.au/131754-heres-how-to-achieve-gender-equality-after-the-pandemic/.

104 Gloria Feldt, "Art and the Zen of Leadership," Take The Lead Women, July 22, 2018, https://www.taketheleadwomen.com/blog/art-and-the-zen-of-leadership.

105 "CEO Sage," Scott Jeffrey, https://scottjeffrey.com/about/.

106 Scott Jeffrey, "How Leaders Use Symbols to Influence Others," Business 2 Community, July 27, 2018, https://www.business2community.com/leadership/how-leaders-use-symbols-to-influence-others-02096894.

107 "Lasso of Truth," Wikipedia, accessed May 25, 2021, https://en.wikipedia.org/wiki/Lasso_of_Truth.

108 Naomi Adedokun, "Meghan Markle's Necklace Holds Hidden 'Symbol' for Daughter as She 'Proudly Displays' Bump," Express, May 12, 2021, https://www.express.co.uk/news/royal/1434984/meghan-markle-fashion-news-duchess-of-sussex-jewellery-latest-video-vax-live-royal-news-vn.

109 Janelle Harris Dixon, "Why the Black National Anthem Is Lifting Every Voice to Sing," Smithsonian Magazine, August 10, 2020, https://www.smithsonianmag.com/smithsonian-institution/why-black-national-anthem-lifting-every-voice-sing-180975519/.

110 amra & elma, https://www.amraandelma.com/.

Chapter 9

111 Jimmie Briggs, "How Black Men Have Helped Erase Black Women's Pain," *Daily Beast*, May 22, 2020, https://www.thedailybeast.com/on-the-record-russell-simmons-and-how-black-men-have-helped-erase-black-womens-pain?ref=author.

112 Tom Murphy, "Lin Manuel Miranda's Feminism Freestyle Is Better than You Imagine," Global Citizen, March 18, 2016, https://www.globalcitizen.org/en/

content/lin-manuel-mirandas-feminism-freestyle-is-better-t/.

113 Jane Wakefield, "The Tech Billionaire Who Is Putting Women First," BBC News, April 7, 2021, https://www.bbc.com/news/technology-56662100.

114 Alix Langone, "#MeToo and Time's Up Founders Explain the Difference between the 2 Movements—And How They're Alike," *Time Magazine*, March 22, 2018, https://time.com/5189945/whats-the-difference-between-the-metoo-and-times-up-movements/.

115 David G. Smith and W. Brad Johnson, "Male Mentors Shouldn't Hesitate to Challenge Their Female Mentees," *Harvard Business Review*, May 29, 2017, https://hbr.org/2017/05/et-yyt-how-some-male-mentors-fail-at-challenging-their-female-mentees.

116 Julie Beck, "Raising Boys with a Broader Definition of Masculinity," *The Atlantic*, April 15, 2019, https://www.theatlantic.com/family/archive/2019/04/how-raise-boys/587107/.

Chapter 10

117 Nick Bastone, "Salesforce's Chief People Officer Explains How and Why the Company Has Spent $8.7 million to Close Its Gender Pay Gap," *Insider*, December 15, 2018, https://www.businessinsider.com/cindy-robbins-salesforce-equal-pay-2018-11#since-an-audit-like-this-had-never-been-conducted-at-salesforce-robbins-and-seka-had-first-to-assemble-a-team-of-internal-and-external-experts-and-define-their-methodology-they-then-assessed-all-of-salesforces-some-30000-employees-and-made-the-necessary-adjustments-to-their-compensation-to-close-the-gap-3.